CP/M®
PRIMER

by

Stephen M. Murtha and Mitchell Waite

Howard W. Sams & Co., Inc.
4300 WEST 62ND ST. INDIANAPOLIS, INDIANA 46268 USA

FIRST EDITION
FOURTH PRINTING—1982

International Standard Book Number: 0-672-21791-0
Library of Congress Catalog Card Number: 80-53271

Printed in the United States of America.

PREFACE

CP/M® (Control Program for Microcomputers) is an extremely popular "disk operating system" for 8080, 8085, and Z80 based microcomputers. Today almost every microcomputer manufacturer that utilizes a floppy disk system for mass storage of programs supplies CP/M as the main operating system for the computer product. A disk operating system "orchestrates" the operation of various programs that may reside on the disk, as well as supervising i/o operations, and performing the various "housekeeping" tasks required by any computer. A program designed to operate with the CP/M operating system can, under most conditions, be run on any other computer that has CP/M. Hence, a huge body of programs exists for CP/M microcomputer owners, and this has in turn attracted ever larger numbers of computer manufacturers to offer CP/M for their computers. With so many people using CP/M on a daily basis, we feel there exists a need for a clearly written book describing the features of the CP/M operating system. This book was written for the purpose of introducing the CP/M disk operating system to the first-time user in a clear, precise, and lucid manner. The book is intended to get you quickly into using and working with CP/M.

Chapters 1 and 2 contain an introduction to microcomputers in general and briefly explain many of the concepts with which a typical user will need to be familiar in order to understand the CP/M operating system. Chapters 3 through 8 describe in detail the operation and capabilities of the CP/M operating system. After you have read these chapters, you should be able to fully use the CP/M operating system in any application. However, many people are not satisfied with simply knowing the mechanics of operating CP/M, but are also curious about *why* CP/M works the way it does. For those people we have included Appendix A, which explains the basic internal operation of CP/M. Many of the concepts which are contained in Appendix A are somewhat difficult, so if you are not feeling up to it, do not despair. Skipping Appendix A will not in any way prevent you from using and enjoying CP/M on your microcomputer.

Appendix B contains a list of software which is CP/M compatible. We hope that if you do not want to do your own programming that you will be able to use this list to secure the software which you need to use your microcomputer for whatever application you desire.

We would like to thank Henry Dakin, Peter Kirkwood, Ken Klein, Michael Belling, Julie Arca, and Philip Lieberman for their assistance in reviewing this manuscript. Their comments were invaluable in helping to make this book hopefully more useful and valuable. In addition, a warm thank you needs to go out to Larry Press and the rest of the gang in Santa

Monica at Small Systems Group for their help in compiling the list of software vendors used in Appendix B. Finally, we would like to acknowledge Bob Gumpertz for the drawings which capture the essence of the concepts which we put forth in the book, and present them in a refreshing manner.

STEPHEN MURTHA
MITCHELL WAITE

CONTENTS

CHAPTER 8

APPENDIX A

APPENDIX B

APPENDIX C

chapter **1**

Introduction to CP/M®*

If this is the first time you've studied CP/M or if you aren't familiar with microcomputer technology and operating systems, you should read this chapter before proceeding further. This chapter introduces the concept of operating systems, briefly describes what a microcomputer is, presents a brief history of CP/M, summarizes the scope of programs available for CP/M systems today, and concludes with a description of how this book is organized.

If you are already familiar with some aspects of CP/M, you can skip this chapter and proceed to Chapter 2, which describes some hardware and software concepts necessary to the understanding of a CP/M microcomputer system (logical and physical i/o, languages, etc.).

In this chapter we will attempt to introduce you to CP/M and give you some idea of what it will do. In the successive chapters we will take a look at each of the features of the CP/M operating system in detail and give you an idea of how to use them. We will include in each of these discussions actual examples of the points we are discussing. The crt outline shown below will be used to show you how an example should appear on the screen of an actual CP/M computer. If you have your own computer or have access to a computer which runs under the CP/M operating system, we encourage you to try on your machine the examples listed in the book.

In Chapter 2 we will look at the hardware of a typical microcomputer and see how CP/M interfaces to it. We will briefly discuss how CP/M is structured internally so that when we are examining some of the more advanced features later on in this book you will know what we are talking about.

Chapter 3 will cover starting up a CP/M system. We will show you what to do when you switch on a computer with the CP/M operating system in it and how to use the basic functions.

---

* CP/M is a registered trademark of Digital Research Inc.

Chapters 4 through 8 cover the numerous utilities which are included in the basic CP/M system. We will cover interrogating the system for its status; creating, moving, and saving data; editing a file with text or a program in it, and assembling and debugging an assembly language program.

Wherever you decide to start, keep in mind that this book is written to help you use CP/M on a real microcomputer. Although you can read the book through like a novel, and undoubtedly glean much data, the book will work best when used in conjunction with a computer running CP/M and the set of operating manuals that comes with the CP/M disks.

Since its inception in 1970 the microprocessor has quietly reshaped our world as we know it. It has enabled "intelligence" to be incorporated into products which we use on an everyday basis, from automobile engines to microwave ovens. In addition to their use in enhancing the capabilities of consumer and industrial products, microprocessors have been used over the past five years as the heart of small, but remarkably powerful, computers. These computers are usually referred to as microcomputers. These microcomputers are being used today in many business applications such as accounting and word processing, in education and research to interpret and compile data, and even in the home as very sophisticated educational and entertainment devices.

How can the microcomputer be used in so many unique end products? The answer is that the microcomputer responds to a unique set of machine instructions, and the way these instructions are grouped or arranged determines how the microprocessor's intelligence is employed, be it as a processor of words, a traffic light controller, or a computer game. It is the flexibility and power of these instructions which give the microprocessor its power and versatility.

As with most things in life, no two microcomputer applications ever seem quite the same. Therefore, one would expect that each microcomputer must have its own unique program to allow it to perform its particular function. To a large extent, this is true. However, each of these individual programs have certain elements that are common. Each program must have sections to input data from some form of console device, print output to a printer, store and retrieve data on a disk, and so on. The common elements of these programs are usually grouped together into what is referred to as an *operating system*. Thus, a programmer can save a tremendous amount of time and energy. By integrating these common elements into the main program via the operating system, the programmer is then free to concentrate on the parts of the program that are unique to the specific application at hand.

In the last 20 years many computer manufacturers have developed operating systems for their particular hardware systems. CP/M is one of the most popular and widely used operating systems for microcomputers. Since its introduction in 1975, CP/M has been used by dozens of manufacturers of microcomputers and has become as close as anything to being the "industry standard." This popularity is no doubt directly related to its ease of operation and flexibility.

WHAT IS AN OPERATING SYSTEM?

For those who have suddenly found themselves caught up in computers and computing, terms such as "operating system," "RAM," "list device," and the like tend to be confusing when they are first encountered. We will make a small digression at this point to explain exactly what an operating system is, why it is necessary, and what it does. Those of you who are already familiar with operating systems may want to read the rest of this section to refresh your memory, or you may want to skip ahead to the next section.

A computer, whether it is a $5000 microcomputer or a multimillion dollar IBM mainframe, is a machine which continuously executes a series of instructions called a program. Although a computer has tremendous capabilities and often appears to have a very fast and efficient human mind, it does not have any of the human characteristics called intuition or deductive reasoning. Thus a computer must be told what to do at all times. The nature of computer design is such that in addition to the requirement that the computer have a program to execute at all times, the steps or sequence of instructions of that program is critical.

In order to illustrate this point a little more clearly, let us assume that you are out for a Sunday drive and you notice that your gas gauge registers a bit on the low side. You pull into the brand new "gas station of the future" which MONOCO (Monolithic Oil Company) has just installed up the street, and you notice that there is

CP/M OPERATING SYSTEM

a computer minding the station instead of the high school kid who used to pump the gas. You roll down your window and say into the computer's grill-like ears "fill'er up," expecting that without further ado your gas tank will be filled with unleaded gas, your oil, radiator, windshield washer, and battery levels will be checked, and your front and back windshields will be cleaned for you just like the old days. Right? Wrong.

To start with the computer, who speaks nothing but the King's English, does not recognize the word "fill'er" as "fill her." However, even if it had it would not have been able to guess what kind of gas to put in the car, although the high school kid would have looked at the car and figured out that since it is a 1978 car it must use unleaded. The computer would not have checked under the hood for you since you didn't ask, and would not have even attempted to clean your windshield since "clean" is such a subjective term.

By this time of course, you have figured out that the only intelligent plan of action at this point is to immediately drive away and find a good ol' fashioned gas station that understands the expression "fill'er up." Of course you could have painstakingly explained in infinite detail to the computer back there at the MONOCO station exactly how to perform all of those tasks, but after all, you wanted to go for a drive on this particular Sunday.

Which brings us to the whole point of this discussion. If you don't tell the computer how to do these things, someone else has to. The whole reason for installing the computer there at MONOCO was to allow you to have your car filled with gas promptly and efficiently. So someone must tell the computer how to perform these basic functions, and that set of instructions is what would be referred to as an operating system. An operating system would know what to do when you said "fill'er up."

Generally, any operating system can be defined as the interface between the computer and the computer user. *Its purpose is to provide the user with a flexible and manageable means of control over the resources of the computer.* The three primary functions fulfilled by all operating systems are:

1. Provide an orderly and consistent input/output (i/o) environment for the various elements of the computer (i.e., terminal, printer, hard or floppy disk, magnetic tape, etc.) to operate in. Input/output is a generalized expression that means responding to a key being depressed on the keyboard, sending a character to the screen or printer, etc.
2. Provide file management and status reporting for the data being stored in the computer system. A file management system will

THE HISTORY OF CP/M

allow a user to find out what files are on a disk, how big the files are, how much unused space is left on the disk, as well as managing the reading and writing of information to and from the disk.

3. Provide for the loading and execution of user programs. Many operating systems have far more elaborate features such as the ability to execute more than one user task at one time, the ability to keep track of the amount of time each user spends on the system, a system of passwords to protect data and programs, etc. However, they all perform the three basic functions mentioned above in one form or another.

THE HISTORY OF CP/M

The microcomputer traces its roots to the first microprocessor, the Intel 4004. The 4004 was first introduced in 1970 and was extremely primitive by standards of today. However, elementary as it was, it was a major advancement in integrated circuit technology. Intel followed the 4004 with the 4040, both of which were 4-bit machines and then the 8008, the first 8-bit microprocessor. Finally, in early 1973 Intel announced the 8080, the first microprocessor which was powerful enough to be used in a microcomputer.

The first real microcomputer, and the one that started the current expansion of small computers, was the MITS Altair. The Altair appeared on the cover of *Popular Electronics* in December of 1974. Its popularity was phenomenal and it caught everyone by surprise. Apparently a huge unperceived market existed for computers in the under $1000 range (the MITS Altair kit went for $375 back then in its most stripped-down version). Soon there were other companies springing up to offer additional computer products that were compatible with the Altair as well as some companies that started making computers to compete with the Altair. Some of the early companies were Imsai, Processor Technology, Cromemco, and North Star. As the hardware offerings of these companies began to round out, initial software offerings in the form of assemblers, disassemblers, and rudimentary BASIC interpreters appeared.

The initial mass storage medium for the early microcomputers was the familiar cassette tape. Most of the companies offered an interface card which allowed the user to attach an ordinary cassette tape recorder to the computer and thereby

What Is a Microcomputer?

When discussing types of computers, the computer industry tends to try to place computers into one of three categories, based on the characteristics and capabilities of the machine. The three categories most frequently used are mainframes, minicomputers, and microcomputers. As technology progresses and more powerful computers appear on the market, the difference between these three types of computers is becoming smaller and smaller to where it is very difficult, if not impossible, to tell them apart.

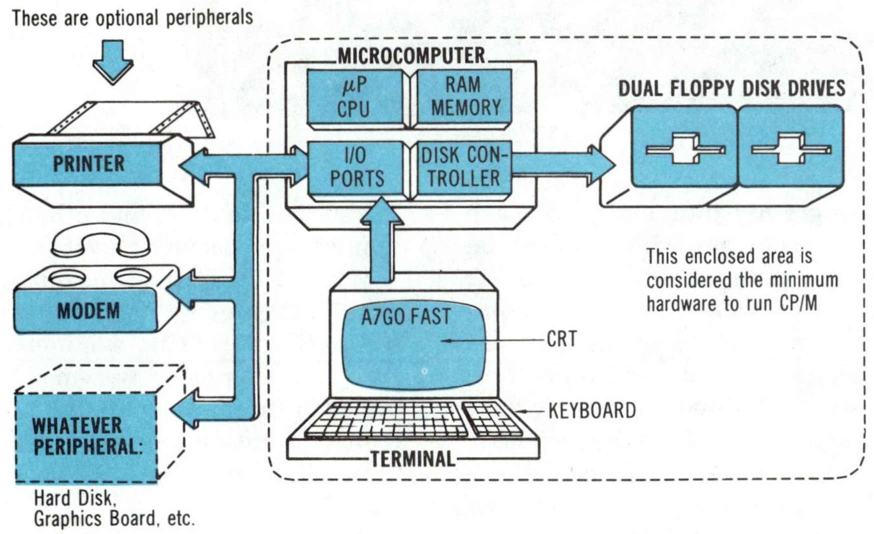

Fig. 1-1. A typical CP/M microcomputer system. Drives should be 8″ single or double density, or 5¼″ double or quad density.

This is the case particularly with microcomputers and minicomputers. For the purposes of this book we will define a microcomputer as a computer based around an 8-bit microprocessor, which can execute a single user's program. Fig. 1-1 shows a typical microcomputer. A minicomputer is a computer that is based on a 16-bit or larger central processor which has the capability to execute the programs of one or more users. The difficulty in distinguishing between mini and microcomputers arises from recent developments in the microprocessor field where 16-bit microprocessors with more power than the 16-bit CPUs (central processing units) of 5 years ago are a reality, and the 32-bit microprocessors are on their way. Thus the mini/micro distinction is becoming more and more artificial.

A mainframe is a very large and sophisticated computer. Mainframes typically will execute the programs of many users at one time at very high rates of speed, and usually have either 32- or 64-bit CPUs. Some mainframes are so fast and powerful that they have to have minicomputers attached to them to do the scheduling of programs through them, and to provide the input/output interface to tape and disk drives, printers, and the like. If these machines had people running the scheduling or if they interfaced directly to the peripherals they would only be able to run at a small fraction of their full potential.

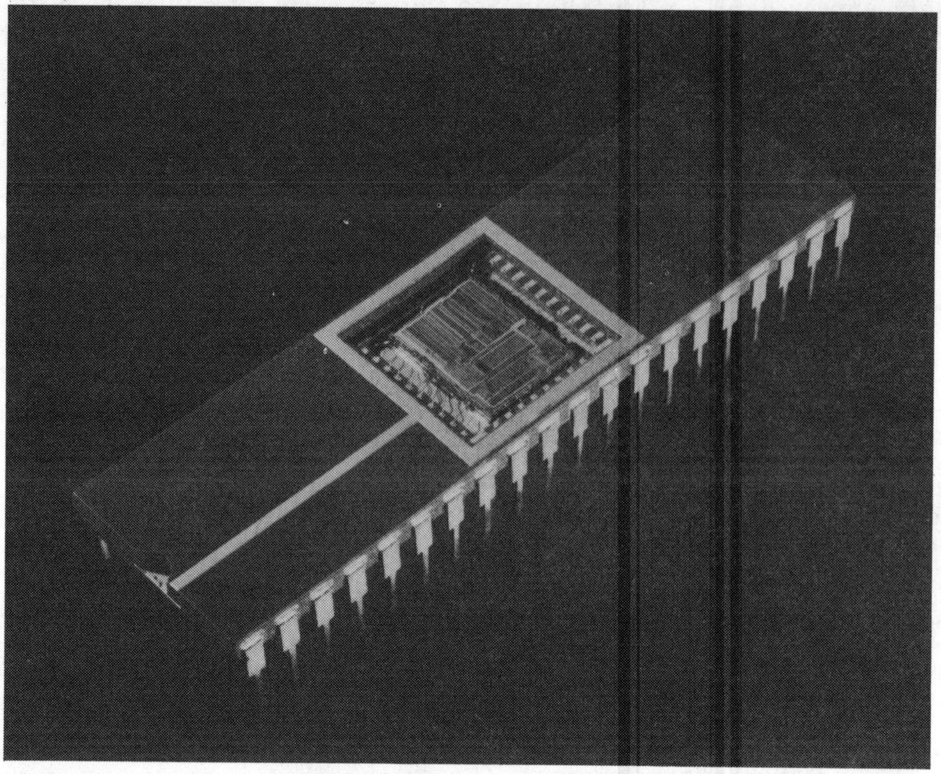

Courtesy Intel Corp.

Fig. 1-2. The 8080 microprocessor for which CP/M was first created.

store and retrieve programs, data, and text. Each company had its own programs which controlled the tape cassette, recording method, and other features. However, there was little or no compatibility between the various recording schemes and formats. Although several attempts were made to create a standard tape storage format (most notably the Kansas City standard), no clear-cut standard ever appeared. Consequently there was very little software transportability between different manufacturers' devices, and programs could not be easily traded or swapped among computer owners.

Soon after the cassette recorder appeared on the market, a few of the more innovative companies introduced a floppy disk based mass storage device. The floppy disk offered a price/performance increase over the cassette of several times. With a floppy disk, a program could be loaded in seconds, instead of minutes and a much larger number of programs could be stored on one diskette than could ever be stored on a cassette.

With the advent of the floppy disk drive, applications for the microcomputer opened up which had not existed previously. With cassette tape as the only mass storage medium, the microcomputer was limited to educational, hobby, and other applications where the limitations imposed by the use of cassette tapes as a mass storage medium could be accepted. However, with the floppy disk, business, scientific, and other higher performance applications became possible.

While all of this was going on, Gary Kildall (the author of CP/M) was working for Intel as a consultant writing a language called PL/M for Intel's development systems. As can best be determined from microcomputer folklore (passed down from generation to generation by the great sages), the development of CP/M went something like this.

At that time, paper tape was the only form of mass storage that had been adapted for microcomputers (consisting mainly at that time of the Intel Intellec development systems). The most commonly used paper tape punch and reader is the Teletype Model 33 telex machine. For those of you who have never used one of these beasts, their particular brand of noisy, slow, mechanical dependability can only be appreciated by those who understand the sublime beauty of a Sherman tank. Fortunately, there are very few people in the microcomputer field who possess this state of mind, and so it is no surprise that Gary found the then recently developed floppy disk drive intriguing.

After securing a floppy disk for himself, Gary realized that a floppy alone does not a mass storage device make. A cabinet, controller, power supply, cables, and programming are also necessary. Thus Gary enlisted the help of his friend John

Torode to complete the project. While Gary developed the file manager (the forerunner of CP/M's BDOS), John completed the disk controller. Finally, all was ready and the first CP/M disk system was a reality.

During the next year or so relatively little interest was shown by the microcomputer industry for CP/M. Intel expressed no interest, and although a few commercial licenses were granted, none of the then dominant microcomputer manufacturers expressed any interest. It was not until Glenn Ewing of Imsai approached Gary for a license that CP/M really began to take off. Out of the dialog with Glenn came the concept of consolidating all of the hardware dependent portions of CP/M in one section, so that anyone could buy a copy of CP/M and do his or her own modification. With this change, the rapid proliferation of CP/M throughout the industry began.

In order to provide the support manufacturers and users would require, Gary started Digital Research in 1976. Since that time, Digital Research has grown and matured with the microcomputer market, and now offers more advanced versions of CP/M, as well as related software products such as a macroassembler (MAC), a symbolic debugger (SID) for debugging assembly language programs, a text formatter (TEX) which can be used with text editors such as ED to produce professional word processor quality text output. More recently, products which support more than one user at a time in the CP/M environment have been announced. No doubt, more products will be announced in the near future from Digital Research.

Gary and Digital Research added an assembler, debugger, text editor, and a number of system utilities to CP/M with time which allowed the user to write programs, store and retrieve data, and in general utilize the full capacity of a microcomputer. However, its most important contribution was that CP/M was not designed around any one manufacturer's hardware but rather, was written so that it could be used, with the proper modifications, on almost any microcomputer. This was a large step forward, since it meant that programmers could develop software such as more sophisticated BASIC interpreters, text editors, and other software in the CP/M environment and be assured that it would run and be available on the hardware of many manufacturers.

WHY CP/M IS SO POPULAR

The CP/M operating system has been around for over five years and during that time a huge number of programs have been written to run under it. There are business programs, educational programs, games, programming aids, high level languages, and other special purpose programs such as data communications programs available for the CP/M environment.

There are over 100 companies offering software products that run under CP/M. Appendix B lists a sampling of these programs as well as the names of companies to write to for more information. Table 1-1 summarizes some of the types of programs currently available which are CP/M compatible. In addition to the programs listed in Table 1-1 and Appendix B, there is a vast number of

WHY IS CP/M SO POPULAR?

games and other entertainment-oriented programs which can be found in computer magazines, computer club newsletters, books, and other commonly available sources.

Table 1-1. Summary of Types of Programs Currently Available That Are CP/M Compatible

LANGUAGES:
● BASIC
● FORTRAN
● COBOL
● PASCAL
SYSTEM UTILITIES:
● MACROASSEMBLERS
● SYMBOLIC DEBUGGERS
● DISASSEMBLERS
● SYSTEM DIAGNOSTICS
● DATA BASE MANAGEMENT SYSTEMS
● SORT/MERGE
APPLICATION PROGRAMS:
● GENERAL LEDGER
● ACCOUNTS PAYABLE
● ACCOUNTS RECEIVABLE
● PAYROLL
● INVENTORY
● ORDER ENTRY
● BUSINESS SIMULATION AND MODELING
● GRAPHICS
● TAX PLANNING AND PREPARATION
● WORD PROCESSING

WHAT IS THE FUTURE FOR CP/M?

During their first five years, CP/M and Digital Research have made a significant contribution to the field of microcomputers, whether for personal or business use. Without the CP/M operating system, and its easy adaptability to many different

computers, the large body of software which is currently available for microcomputers would not be nearly as large or as sophisticated as it currently is.

Two recent products announced by Digital Research can give us some idea of what is in store for microcomputers and CP/M during the next five years. MP/M and CP/Net are the two products and both represent the current focus in the industry toward distributed processing and microcomputer networks. Exciting as microcomputers have been in the past five years, they have been limited to single-user applications. The possibilities of applications involving microcomputers accessing large common data bases or microcomputers strung together into large networks are truly mind-boggling. The next five years show incredible promise for CP/M, MP/M, and CP/Net as microcomputer programmers begin to explore the capabilities of microcomputers joined together into ever larger and more sophisticated networks.

chapter 2

A CP/M Microcomputer: Hardware and Software Concepts

Throughout this book we will be talking about microcomputers and we will be using several technical terms to describe them. In order to fully understand the concepts we are presenting, we will take a moment here to explain in detail some of these terms and concepts. If you are already familiar with microcomputers you may wish to skip this chapter entirely.

CENTRAL PROCESSING UNIT (CPU)

All computers have three main types of components in them. The first is the central processing unit (abbreviated CPU). This is the brain or the smarts of the computer, and in microcomputers, the wizards of Silicon Valley (Santa Clara County, California) have reduced it into one small integrated circuit. There are many types of CPUs and they vary in how much work they will do and how fast they will do that work. The particular CPU which CP/M was first written for was the Intel 8080. Since the original introduction of the Intel 8080, two more CPUs have entered the market which are for the most part compatible with the 8080 and on which CP/M will run. These newer CPUs are the Intel 8085 and the Zilog Z80.

Each of these CPUs has its own instruction set. An instruction set is simply the total repertoire of commands which the CPU will recognize and execute. The 8085 and Z80 execute a superset of the basic 8080 set and so in order to have CP/M run on all of these CPUs, Digital Research has written CP/M using only the 8080 instruction set. While the 8080, 8085, and Z80 all execute the same 8080 instruction set, the 8085 and Z80 CPUs operate at roughly twice the speed of the 8080. Because of this, the microcomputers which are being sold today use almost exclusively 8085 and Z80 CPUs in them.

MEMORY

The second major component of a computer is its memory. Memory is that part of the computer in which programs and data are stored. There are many types of computer memory. There is the internal memory that the computer uses for storing the programs and data which it must execute immediately, such as the current program. There is also mass external storage, for storing files and large amounts of data that are not required immediately by the computer for execution. Internal memory is either random access memory (RAM) or read only memory (ROM). RAM is used where data or program steps must be stored and easily changed. RAM comprises the largest portion of the internal memory in a typical computer installation. ROM, on the other hand, is used for small programs which are not changed at all. The initializing program which is executed as soon as the computer is turned on is usually stored in ROM. CP/M operates in the RAM section of the computer's memory, although it is stored on the floppy disk, so that it is preserved when the power is turned off, since the contents of a computer's RAM memory are lost when power is removed.

INPUT/OUTPUT

Input/output or i/o is the third major component of the computer. This is the portion of the computer which allows it to communicate with the outside world. Typical i/o devices which are attached to a computer are printers, crt terminals, paper tape punches, punched card readers, etc. Fig. 2-1 shows a typical microcomputer configuration with the CPU, memory and i/o sections marked. A microcomputer accomplishes this i/o with the outside world through channels which are called ports. The physical addresses of the i/o ports vary from computer to computer. CP/M gives them logical titles (crt, LST, etc.) and BIOS is modified for the differences. Each port has its own unique address, very much like the memory in the microcomputer is broken up into individually numbered addresses. The i/o ports are numbered 1 to 256 in a microcomputer running CP/M. As you can see from Fig. 2-1, the devices such as printers, crt terminals and the like are attached to the i/o ports. For example, the crt in Fig. 2-1 may be attached to port 12. Thus, to move data to and from the crt, the CPU must move characters in and out of port 12. If the CPU tried to move data in and out of any other port, nothing would show up on the screen, and the computer would appear to ignore the keyboard input.

LOGICAL AND PHYSICAL I/O

While Fig. 2-1 shows a typical system, it is by no means the only configuration available. A microcomputer can have multiple printers attached or almost any combination of the i/o devices listed above. One of the purposes of CP/M is to eliminate the need for the programmer to worry about the exact i/o configuration of the particular microcomputer which the program is to run on. One of the most common methods of eliminating this problem is the creation of what are referred to as "logical" i/o devices which the programmer may program for.

The opposite of a "logical" device is not an illogical device, but rather a "physical" device. A physical i/o device is the actual i/o device, whereas a logical i/o device is the programming representation we make of that physical device.

Although this may sound like an awkward way of doing things at first glance, we actually use this logical/physical relationship all of the time in day-to-day life. For example, where do you go when you leave work each day? You go home, of course. Well when someone asks you where are you going you tell them you are going "home." Now the truth of the matter is that you live at 123 Main St. Anytown, USA just like every other John Doe. But isn't it so much easier to tell people that you are going "home" than you are going to "123 Main St. Anytown, USA." And if you have followed us this far you should also now see that "home" is where you have referred to for each

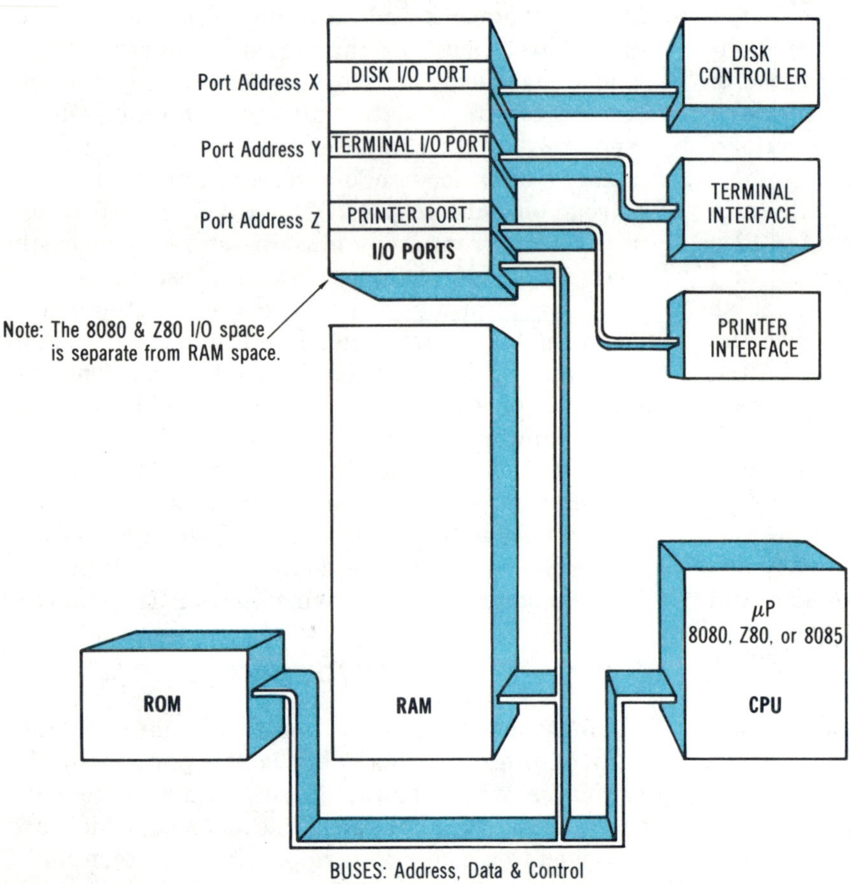

Fig. 2-1. Logical and physical i/o.

LOGICAL and PHYSICAL I/O

of the ten places you have lived throughout your life. Thus, although your actual address changes, your response to the philosophical question of "where are you going" doesn't. Now doesn't that make life that much easier?

With CP/M this concept of logical devices is not only nice, it is a necessity. Since there are versions of CP/M for over 100 different computers, CP/M must allow programs to simply say "send this home" and know that the particular version of CP/M which is running on that machine will translate that into "send this to 123 Main Street Anytown, USA" or "send this to 999 Square Street Nowheresville, USA" or whatever is appropriate. This translation is done for the programmer by CP/M.

Thus if a program sends information to the crt screen it will say, in essence "output to screen" (perhaps via a statement like PRINT in BASIC). Your particular version of CP/M has been customized (usually by the manufacturer of your computer) so it interprets "output to screen" correctly and sends the information to the correct physical place in the computer's structure to accomplish this command.

CP/M has four logical i/o devices that it talks to. They are the CONSOLE device, the LIST device, the PUNCH device, and the READER device. Of these, the PUNCH and READER devices are very rarely used in actual day-to-day applications. They are used to punch and read paper tapes. With the advent of relatively low-cost floppy disk drives, paper tape is seldom used as a storage medium. For this reason we will ignore the PUNCH and READER devices and concentrate on the CONSOLE and LIST devices throughout the rest of the book. However, understand that you may occasionally see READER and PUNCH used for some other i/o device than paper tape.

The CONSOLE device is the device through which the operator makes his or her wishes known to the computer. The CONSOLE logical device is usually a crt terminal, although almost any device that allows two-way communication with the computer may be used. The LIST device is the principal output device used for hard-copy (a fancy name for paper) output, such as a printer.

MACHINE LANGUAGE

CP/M has been written to run on either an 8080, 8085, or Z80 microprocessor. The actual CP/M program is written in 8080 machine language, but since both the 8085 and Z80 will execute 8080 machine language as well as certain instructions of their own, CP/M may be run on those computers. If all of this talk about machine language, instruction sets, and the like has you slightly confused at this point don't panic. We will deal with the topic only peripherally at this point. We will talk in much more detail about all of this in Chapters 7 and 8 when we discuss the CP/M Assembler (ASM) and Dynamic Debugging Tool (DDT) in detail.

When talking about progamming, there are usually three classes of programs recognized by

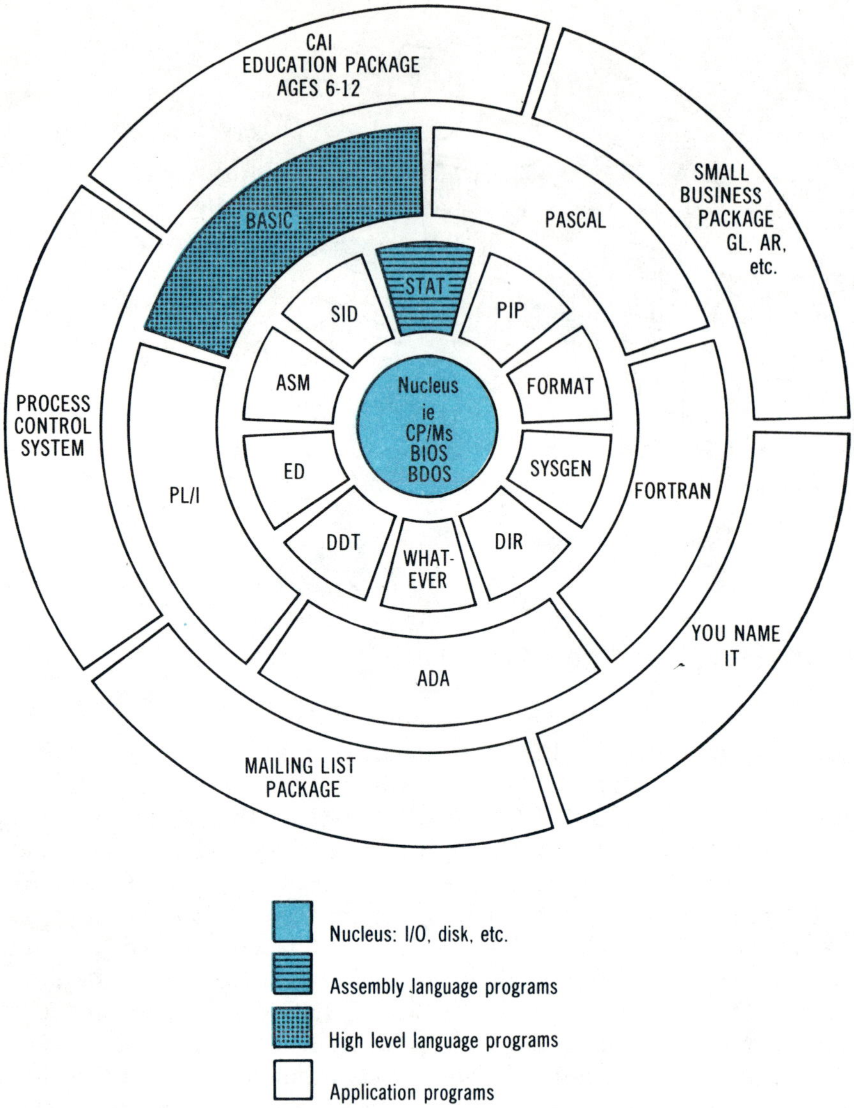

Fig. 2-2. The software hierarchy as seen in a CP/M system.

users, programmers, and the like. They are assembly languages, high level languages, and application programs. The differences between these levels of programming are somewhat arbitrary, but are based on a hierarchy shown in Fig. 2-2. As you can see from the diagram, an operating system of one kind or another is required to perform i/o and system-oriented functions. Assembly language programs are the next level of programs, followed by high level language interpreters, and finally, application programs.

ASSEMBLY LANGUAGE

This is programming at its most basic level. Assembly languages are the first level of programming that must be done for any machine. All programs written in assembler are written using the native instructions of the particular central processor which the computer is based upon. In the case of CP/M of course, this is the 8080, 8085, or Z80 instruction sets. Fig. 2-3 shows a portion of a sample program written in 8080 Assembler. Again, don't worry if it looks like hieroglyphics to you. We will discuss the specifics of reading an assembly language program listing as well as explain the use of a machine language assembler.

HIGH LEVEL LANGUAGES

The next level of programming is referred to as high level languages. These are the languages that programs are written in which are not machine dependent. In other words they are not written to utilize the instruction set of any one CPU. Languages such as BASIC, FORTRAN, COBOL, PASCAL, and others are referred to as high level languages. Most programming is done in these languages, rather than in assembler. The reasons for this are twofold.

```
DIRECT: CALL  FOPEN      ;OPEN FILE
        ;
        LXI   D,DIR$BUF
        CALL  FSETBUF    ;SET NEW BUFFER
        PUSH  D
        ;
        MVI   L,3        ;LOAD COUNTER
        CALL  FREAD      ;MOVE FIRST RECORD
        ;
LOOP4:  POP   D          ;GET DISK BUFFER
        PUSH  H          ;GET REG L OUT OF
                         ;THE WAY
        LXI   H,128
        DAD   D          ;ADD 128 TO DISK
                         ;BUFFER AND SAVE
        XCHG             ;AS NEW BUFFER
        CALL  FSETBUF
        ;
        POP   H          ;GET REG L BACK
        PUSH  D          ;SAVE NEW BUFFER
        CALL  FREAD      ;READ NEXT RECORD
        ;
        DCR   L
        JNZ   LOOP4      ;TEST FOR MORE
```

Fig. 2-3. Assembly language program listing. Here the language is for the 8080 microprocessor.

```
10   INPUT "ENTER TWO NUMBERS",X,Y
20   PRINT "ENTER 1 TO ADD"
30   PRINT "         2 TO SUBTRACT"
40   PRINT "         3 TO MULTIPLY"
50   PRINT "         4 TO DIVIDE"
60   INPUT I
70   REM- - -BRANCH TO PROPER OPERATION
80   ON I GOTO 100,200,300,400
90   REM- - -ANYTHING ELSE CAUSES PROGRAM
     TO END
95   GOTO 900
100  REM- - -ADDITION
110  LET Z=X+Y
120  GOTO 500
200  REM- - -SUBRTACTION
210  LET Z=X-Y
220  GOTO 500
300  REM- - -MULTIPLICATION
310  LET Z=X*Y
320  GOTO 500
400  REM- - -DIVISION
410  LET Z=X/Y
500  REM- - -PRINT THE ANSWER AND DO IT
     AGAIN
510  PRINT "THE ANSWER IS";Z
520  GOTO 10
900  END
```

Fig. 2-4. High level language program listing. Here the language is BASIC.

First, high level languages are easier to program in. Single statements in these languages often take hundreds of machine language instructions to implement. Thus the programmer saves tremendous amounts of time, as well as reducing the number of mistakes which will eventually have to be tracked down and corrected. There is a penalty for this however. In assembly languages, the central processor executes the instructions directly. With high level languages, a set of machine level instructions interprets the instructions in the high level language and in effect translates them into machine level instructions. This means that an application which is programmed in a high level language is going to execute much more slowly than the same program written in assembler. Fig. 2-4 shows a portion of a program written in BASIC. Notice that without even knowing anything about the structure and the syntax of a BASIC program, you can still figure out, without too much work, what this program is supposed to do (come on, I know you can). (O.K., you can't . . . it simulates a pocket calculator.)

The second reason for programming in a high level language is the transportability from one computer to another computer of the program (this idea of machine independence). The BASIC program listed in Fig. 2-4 could be run on almost any computer, regardless of the central processor, which has a BASIC language interpreter written for it which adheres to the ANSI standard for BASIC. As a matter of fact, this last feature of high level languages is so important that each of the major high level languages has a standard so that the interpreters offered by each manufacturer on their particular central processor will all be the same. The American National Standards Institute (abbreviated ANSI) maintains the standards for BASIC, FORTRAN, and COBOL, which are by far the three most commonly used high level languages.

APPLICATION PROGRAMS

The final level of programming is application programs. These are the programs that perform the desired task for the end user. Typical application programs are accounts receivable processing, order entry, inventory control, and the like. Fig. 2-5 shows the operator's screen for a typical

```
              GENERAL LEDGER MASTER MENU

1-STATUS                   REPORTS:

2-INPUT TRANSACTIONS       7-CHART OF ACCOUNTS
3-EDIT LIST                8-TRIAL BALANCE
4-POST TRANSACTIONS        9-JOURNALS
                           10-REGISTERS
5-END OF MONTH             11-GENERAL LEDGER
6-FILE MAINTENANCE         12-FINANCIAL STATEMENTS

             WHICH OPTION WOULD YOU LIKE?
```

Fig. 2-5. Application program output.

application program. Here the program is presented to the user as a "menu" from which to choose a particular general ledger function for a small business. Application programs are typically written in one of the common high level languages although some are also written in pure assembly and many are a combination of high level and assembly language. They are often written so that one or more programs interact, creating a larger and more sophisticated system than if all tasks were performed separately from each other. A good example of this is an accounting system where the general ledger, accounts receivables, accounts payables, payroll, inventory, order entry, and word processing are all tied together into one large system.

FURTHER READING

We will cover some additional concepts relating to microcomputer systems in other sections of the book. As we explain in greater detail how CP/M works, you will gain further insight into the internal workings of a microcomputer.

This book will not, however, make you an expert in microcomputers. Before you panic, please realize that it is not necessary for you to become an expert in the internal workings of microcomputers to own, use, and enjoy one. We will bring you to that stage during the course of this book. If, on the other hand, you are very anxious to learn more about the internal goings-on of a typical microcomputer and computers in general, then we would like to encourage you to seek out one or more of the many books written on microcomputer basics. Not only will a greater knowledge of computers make CP/M that much easier to understand, but it will introduce you to the many exciting applications that microcomputers are currently opening up. Happy reading!

chapter **3**

Starting Up and First Using a CP/M System

In order to start using CP/M, you must first secure the use of a microcomputer which has a version of CP/M already installed on it. By this, we mean that the manufacturer of the microcomputer has already licensed CP/M from Digital Research, and distributes a copy of CP/M (with the BIOS module already modified for that microcomputer) with every machine that he sells. This is the usual method for a user to get a copy of CP/M. If for some reason, the manufacturer of your microcomputer does not distribute the CP/M operating system, there is a possibility that you may buy a copy of CP/M already modified for your microcomputer from one of several software companies (the most prominent being Lifeboat Associates in New York) who sell CP/M with the BIOS module already modified for a particular brand of microcomputer. If this does not work then you have trouble. You must purchase a copy of CP/M from Digital Research, and modify it for your particular microcomputer. This, unfortunately, is not an easy task. You will also be on your own as far as this book is concerned, since an explanation of the steps required to modify BIOS is beyond the scope of this book.

From this point on, we will be giving examples of the CP/M operating system in actual use. If you own or have access to a microcomputer with CP/M already installed on it, we encourage you to actually do the examples we give on the computer. We will show you what to expect on the screen or printer as output, and what you should input so that you will be able to re-create the examples we have listed. (If you don't have CP/M you can still read the chapter, but you'll have to accept that CP/M outputs the way we show it.)

The first thing you must always do when you start the computer up is load CP/M into the computer's memory so that it can begin executing it. (Remember, CP/M is nothing more than a very special assembly language program, and as we discussed in Chapter 1, a computer always needs an operating system program to execute in order to do anything useful.) Almost all microcomputers have some sort of very primitive program stored in ROM or PROM (so that it will be there when the power is turned off and then turned back on again) which will do things such as examine and change locations in memory, and input and output bytes from the computer ports. This program is referred to as the "monitor" or "executive." Most manufacturers also include in the monitor the ability to load an operating system program from the disk into the computer's memory. This process is referred to as "booting the system," or "bootstrapping the system."

Booting CP/M, and other similar operating systems for that matter, usually remains a mystery for most people. Therefore, let's digress for a while and learn more about it.

BOOTING A CP/M SYSTEM

As we explained earlier in the book, an operating system is the program that, among other things, allows the computer to read and write data and other programs from a mass storage device such as a floppy disk drive. A program, such as an operating system, is necessary to allow this function to be performed. So we have a bit of a Catch-22 here; in order to get the operating system off the disk and into the microcomputer memory when we turn the power on, the operating system must already be in memory! The solution to this problem is the "bootstrap loader."

A microcomputer can be built in such a way that it reads the first sector of the first track of a disk drive into the lowest memory locations every time power is turned off and then on, or the RESET switch is depressed. If a small program is stored on the disk in Track 0, Sector 1, which in turn loads in a larger program (the operating system), then we can get around this problem. This is shown in Figs. 3-1A and 3-1B.

Once the CP/M system is booted, it will display the screen shown at the top of the next page. This will mean that CP/M is reserving the first xxK bytes of memory for its use and the use of programs under its control. Here xx will be

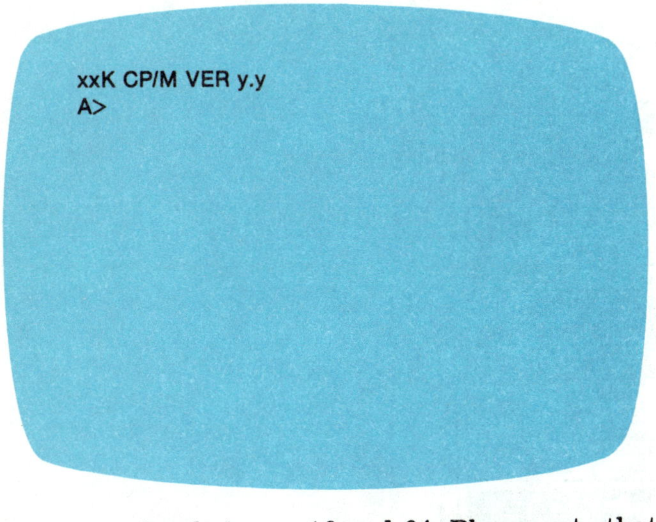

some number between 16 and 64. Please note that it is possible to have more RAM in your computer than the number specified in xx. It is not uncommon to find people using a 32K or 48K CP/M system in a computer with 64K of RAM. Y.y is the version number of the particular type of CP/M being used. As we are writing this book, the latest version number for CP/M is 2.2. There will undoubtedly be new versions of CP/M with time, and all of the information contained in the examples may not be completely correct for your particular version. However, don't despair. In most cases your CP/M manual will explain whatever differences there might be between the various versions. Enough said.

This process of booting is called a "cold boot." It is very similar to starting a cold car in the morning; it was not running recently enough to do us any good. A cold boot on a microcomputer happens after the power has been turned off and then back on. The other type of boot is, oddly enough, a "warm boot," which happens after we run a program or utility and exit back to CP/M and the CCP. As we saw, a cold boot reads in the whole CP/M operating system. A warm boot, on the other hand, reads in only a portion of CP/M. The rest of CP/M is assumed to be intact since there has been no power down, and the program or utility if operating properly, will not alter the memory containing the other part of the CP/M operating system.

CP/M MEMORY USAGE AND ORGANIZATION

As we discussed in Chapter 1, a microcomputer has three basic components; the CPU, the memory, and the i/o ports. In all CP/M computers, the maximum amount of memory which the CPU can address is 65,536 bytes. (This will be denoted as 64K throughout the remainder of the book where K = 1024.) What we mean by this is that every memory location has an address, just like the ones that the Post Office gives us. They are numbered consecutively from 0 to 65,536. This allows the programmer to issue commands such

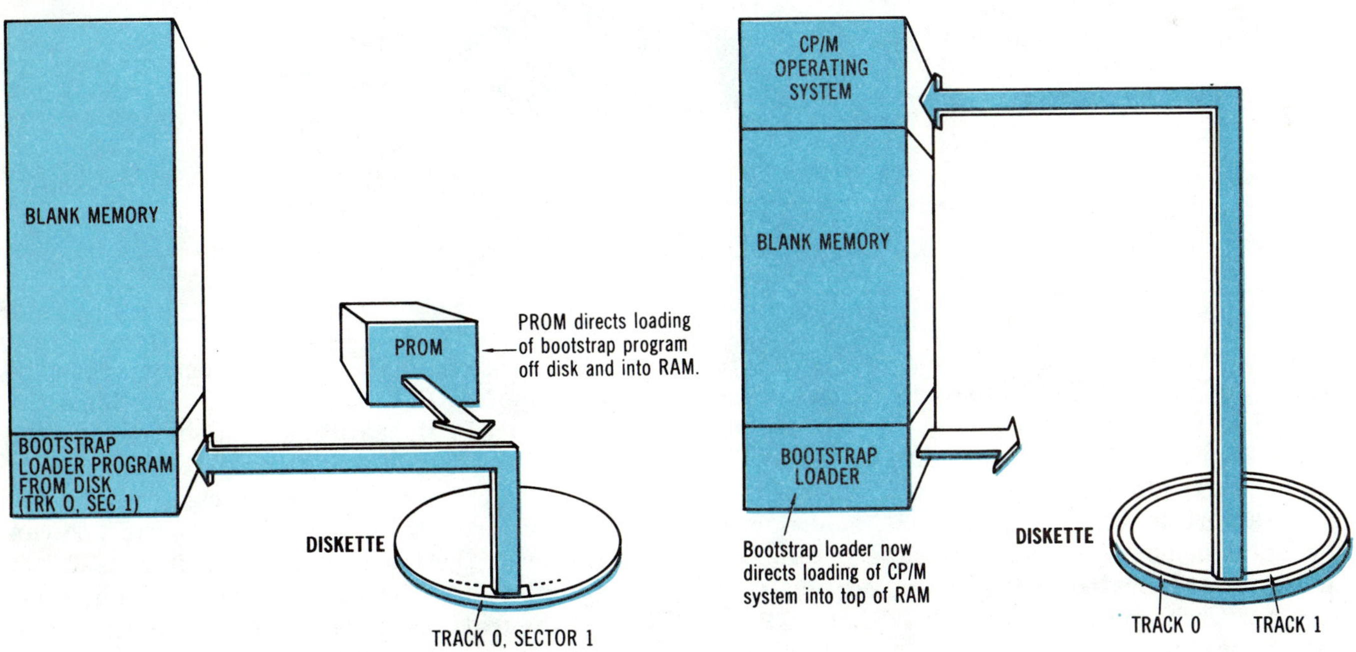

(A) Reading Track 0, Sector 1 into low RAM—CP/M bootstrap program.

(B) Reading all sectors of Tracks 0 and 1 into upper RAM—CP/M system.

Fig. 3-1. Bootstrapping CP/M into RAM.

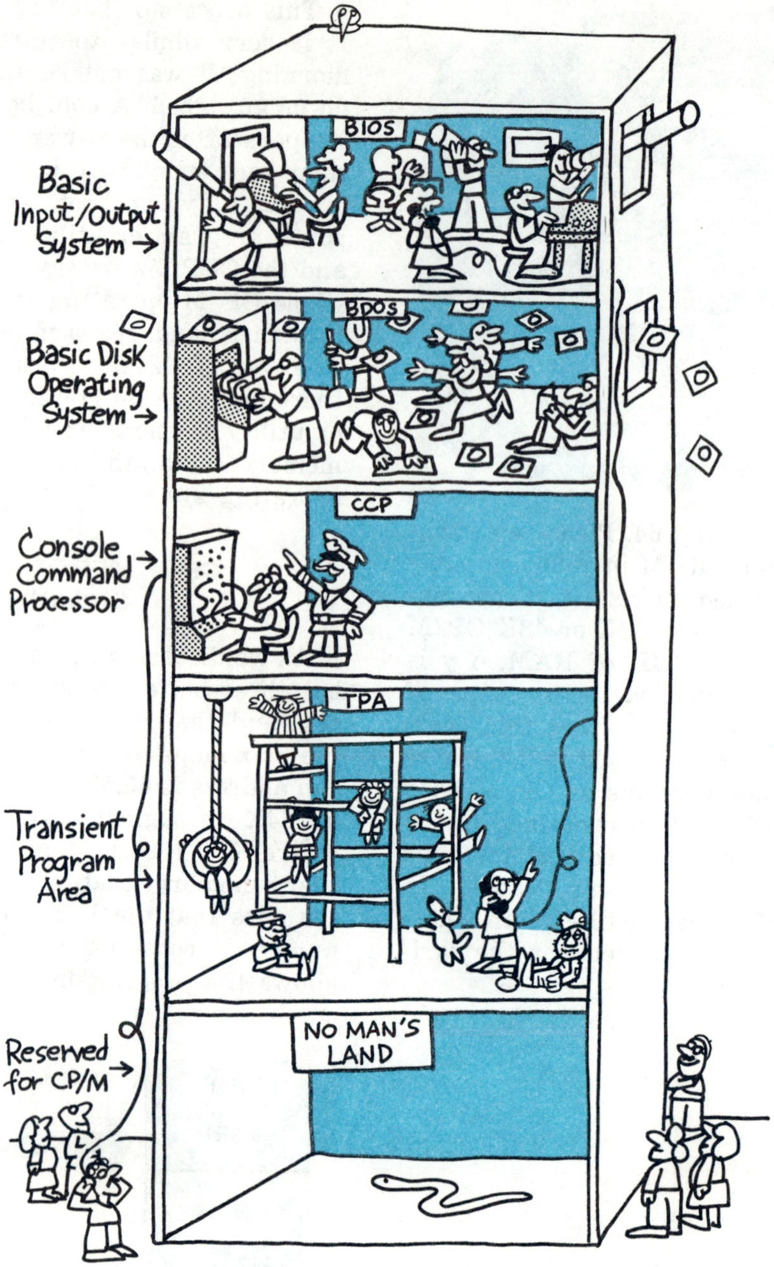

CP/M MEMORY USAGE

as "copy the byte of information at 1,253 into 45,892" and allows the CPU to easily execute these commands.

The CP/M operating system divides the available memory into a number of distinct blocks and reserves certain specific areas for its own use. The only memory locations which are reserved for CP/M are located in the lowest portion (the section with the lowest addresses) so that a CP/M system may be run on a microcomputer system containing anywhere from 16K bytes to 64K bytes of main memory. Fig. 3-2 shows the memory layout of a 64K microcomputer running under CP/M.

If there is less than 64K of main memory, then the TOP OF MEMORY address is lower. Since the size of the CP/M operating system remains the same, the way CP/M adjusts to different amounts of memory is by expanding or compressing the amount of memory allocated for programs to run in. However, there are times when it is useful to store and run a program outside of this area. One of the features of the CP/M operating system is its ability to run under many different combinations of memory and i/o devices. Thus it is perfectly acceptable to have CP/M occupy the first 42K of main memory and have a 24K program

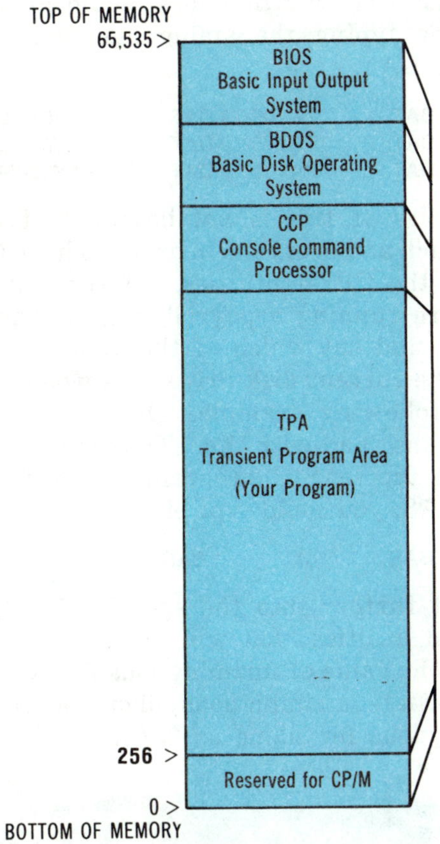

Fig. 3-2. Memory layout for CP/M in a 64K byte system. All of memory is used by CP/M.

reside in the upper memory. Fig. 3-3 shows this.

This flexibility of location in memory is supervised by the MOVCPM utility. At this point it will suffice to say MOVCPM takes each of the individual modules in the CP/M operating system (BDOS, BIOS, and CCP) and modifies them in such a way as to allow them to operate in the locations which they will be occupying in the new size system. Chapter 4 will deal in depth with SYSGEN and MOVCPM, the two utilities which are used to modify and move CP/M systems.

Transient Program Area (TPA)

The TPA is very simply the area in main memory, between memory location 256D or 0100H, the top of the lower memory reserved for CP/M, and the bottom of BDOS. It is where user programs are stored and executed under CP/M. CP/M loads user programs into this area starting at location 0100H and works upward, filling bytes until either the program is completely loaded, or the system is out of memory available for the TPA. You will note that the diagram of the CP/M memory allocation (Fig. 3-2) shows a line between them. However the TPA and the CCP can overlap each other. Whenever a program is too large to reside only in the TPA, CP/M will load a program right over the CCP in order to gain the additional room needed for the program. When the program has finished and wishes to return control to the CCP, the CCP is reloaded from the disk in what is referred to as a "warm boot." The TPA's size varies with the amount of available RAM in your computer. CCP, BDOS, and BIOS are fixed in size.

CCP (Console Command Processor)

The CCP is the portion of CP/M which controls all of the interaction with the operator in the "command" mode of operation, i.e., when a user program is not running and in control of the computer. We will deal with the CCP in more detail further on in the chapter when we talk about resident commands. For now we will leave it that the CCP is the part of CP/M which allows programs to be loaded into the TPA and run, files to be listed, created, deleted, and other "housekeeping" functions performed.

BDOS (Basic Disk Operating System)

BDOS is the portion of the CP/M which handles all of the basic disk file transactions such as reading and writing a record from or to a disk, the dynamic allocation and deallocation of disk space, and other disk-oriented tasks. BDOS, un-

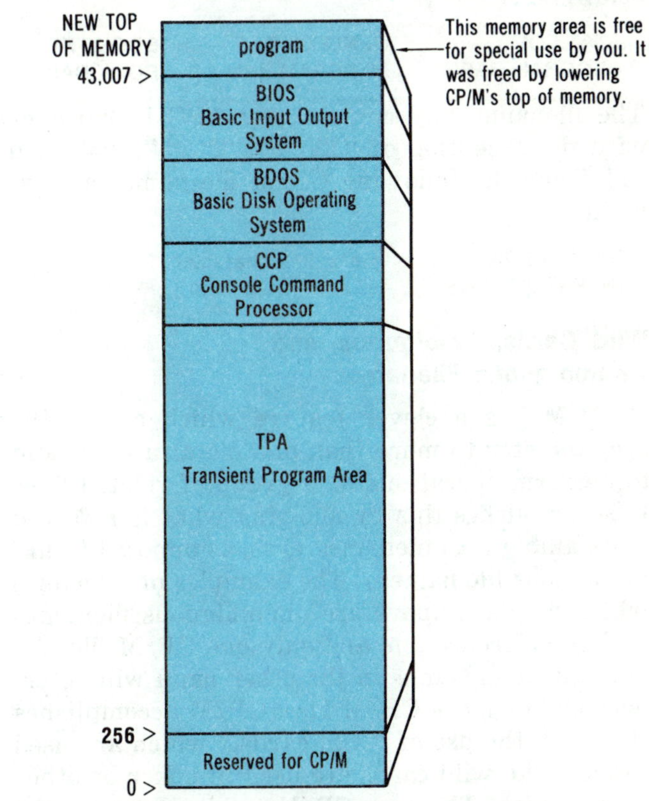

Fig. 3-3. A memory arrangement for CP/M where a free memory area is obtained above BDOS.

like BIOS, is entirely machine-independent; in other words, BDOS is the same for all microcomputers, regardless of the particular disk drive interface or the particular combination of input and output devices hooked up to the computer. BDOS may be considered the core, or the heart, of CP/M.

BIOS (Basic Input/Output System)

BIOS is the third major subsection of the CP/M operating system. BIOS contains all of the programming in CP/M that is machine-dependent. Thus it is in BIOS that all input/output programs (such as those for the console device, the disk controller interface, and the list device) are contained. It is through the BIOS/BDOS concept that as many microcomputers as there are are able to all run CP/M.

CP/M FILES

The beauty of CP/M, and one reason for its popularity is its file handling ability. A file is any collection of data, text, or program instructions which is stored on a floppy disk. All files are referenced by an eight character "filename" and a three character "file type" designator or extension. Examples of valid CP/M filenames are given below.

STAT.COM	GENLEDG.DAT	BOOK.TXT
PROGRAM.BAS	PROGRAM.PRN	BOOK.BAK

The filename may contain any ASCII character with the exception of "?", "*", ".", ",", "=", and ":". Thus the following CP/M file names are invalid.

PAY12:79.DAT	Uses the character ":"
INVENTORY.BAS	Filename too long

Wild Cards, Ambiguous, and Unambiguous Filenames

CP/M has a clever feature which allows the user to refer to more than one file at a time, and to perform operations on a group of related files. It accomplishes this by allowing what is referred to as ambiguous filenames (yes, as opposed to unambiguous file names). The examples of filenames which we gave above are unambiguous filenames —they reference one and only one CP/M file. An ambiguous filename on the other hand will reference one or more CP/M files. CP/M accomplishes this with the use of "wild cards," which are used exactly like wild cards are used in poker or other card games. The two CP/M wild cards are the characters "*" and "?". The "?" character means "match any character" in this location in the filename. Thus the following files would all be referenced by typing the ambiguous filenames of PAY??-79.DAT

PAY01-79.DAT	PAY02-79.DAT	PAY03-79.DAT
PAY04-79.DAT	PAY05-79.DAT	PAY06-79.DAT
PAY07-79.DAT	PAY08-79.DAT	PAY09-79.DAT

The utility of this is not having to type the name of each and every file in order to have CP/M, or one of the CP/M utilities, reference it. Thus if you were running a payroll program and you wanted to find out which of the above data files were on the current disk drive, you would simply type the following example. The "*" wild card simply means "pad with '?'s." Thus if you wanted to find all the BASIC program files with a file type of .BAS, you could type either

????????.BAS   or   *.BAS

As we get further into the specific CP/M commands and utilities, you will begin to see more and more the value of unambiguous filenames. We will abbreviate unambiguous filename as "ufn" and ambiguous file name as "afn."

```
A>DIR PAY??-79.DAT

PAY01-79.DAT
PAY02-79.DAT
PAY03-79.DAT
PAY04-79.DAT
PAY05-79.DAT
PAY06-79.DAT
PAY07-79.DAT
PAY08-79.DAT
PAY09-79.DAT

A>[]
```

File Types

There are several file types which have a special meaning to either CP/M or one or more of the standard CP/M utilities, or one of the high level languages and other programs available for use with CP/M. In order to avoid confusion at a later date, it is best to use the following file types for their specific purpose only. This way you will not be surprised later on when you want to erase all BASIC program source code files from the disk and you have forgotten that some time before you gave the only copy of a valuable text file the file type .BAS. Here are the accepted extensions for CP/M.

.ASM	ASM source code
.BAK	ED generated backup
.BAS	BASIC-E, CBASIC, or MBASIC source code
.CRF	Relocatable assembler cross-reference
.COB	COBOL source
.DAT	ASCII Data (FORTRAN default)
.FOR	FORTRAN source code
.INT	BASIC-E, CBASIC object code
.MAC	Relocatable assembler source
.LST	BASIC-E, CBASIC listing
.OVR	COBOL compiler overlay
.PRN	Listing (assembler, FORTRAN, COBOL, etc.)
.REL	Relocatable object (Relocatable assembler, FORTRAN, etc.)
.SUB	SUBMIT command file
.SYM	Assembler Symbol Table
.XRF	Absolute assembler cross-reference table
.$$$	ED or PIP temporary file

Dynamic File Allocation

A file under CP/M can be as short as zero bytes of data, or as large as the total amount of space available on a disk. One of the functions of the BDOS module in CP/M is the management and allocation of disk space for the files. As a file gets larger, CP/M allocates additional space on the disk for that particular file. This is all very straightforward. However, what sets CP/M apart from some of the other operating systems available is its ability to reclaim allocated space from a file as that file gets smaller. This process of assigning disk space as a file gets larger, and reclaiming disk space as a file gets smaller is called dynamic file allocation.

The actual mechanics of the CP/M dynamic file allocation are very similar to the way a typical business establishment files its records. The disk can be equated with a file cabinet, and a file with a certain drawer in that file cabinet. Thus if you would like to get the payroll records for July, you go to the file cabinet with the payroll records in it (place the payroll disk in the disk drive), and open the drawer marked "July Records" (access the file PAY07-79.DAT). Once inside the drawer of the file cabinet you will find a series of folders, each of which contains some amount of data. CP/M breaks its files up into "records" of 128 bytes per record. Thus a file can have as many records in it as necessary, up to the amount of available space on the disk, just as you can have as many folders in a drawer of a file cabinet as it will physically hold. CP/M will allow you to ask for the 15th record in file PAY07-79.DAT. It will then transfer the 128 bytes of information in that record into the microcomputer memory where it can be examined and/or changed, and then CP/M will transfer the record containing the new information back to the 15th record of PAY07-79.DAT.

CP/M keeps track of where all of the records in a given file are on the disk in a special location also on the disk called the directory. The directory has an entry for each of the files on the disk, which tells how long each of the files is, and where it is located on the disk. Files are created or erased on a disk by either writing or erasing a directory entry.

RESIDENT COMMANDS

The CCP is the portion of CP/M that most users will have the most interaction with. Thus we will spend some time here discussing some of the things that the CCP can do for you.

CP/M will execute two types of commands, resident and transient. Resident commands are the commands whose programs are permanently resident in the CCP and may be used at any time. Transient commands are commands whose programs are stored on a disk. Transients may or may not be called upon at any time, depending on whether they are present on the disk currently in the system. In order to help further distinguish between the two, transient commands are usually called system utilities.

CP/M provides several resident commands for the user. These commands are interpreted and immediately executed by the CCP. The CCP alerts the user to its readiness, willingness, and ability to jump to the user's aid by displaying what is called the "prompt." The prompt is a rather innocuous little thing that appears on the console screen as shown below. The letter "A" with the "greater than" symbol lets the user know that disk A is the "current" disk, that is the disk which will be assumed to be referenced until further notice, and that it is ready to accept a command.

```
A>[ ]
```

(Following the prompt A> is the cursor [ ] which is where the next character will appear when we strike a key.)

THE CONSOLE COMMAND PROCESSOR

CP/M assumes that the disk from which the operating system was booted is the A disk, and that the A disk is the disk "currently" being addressed. The other drives in the system are referenced B, C, D, etc. The A> tells us that subsequent CP/M commands will assume the A drive is the drive which you would like referenced. In order to change the current disk to one of the other disks in the system the user simply types the following

```
A>B:
B>[ ]
```

Typing B: says "switch to drive B:" to CP/M. CP/M will return with the B> prompt to let the user know that drive B is now the current drive.

A word of caution is in order at this point. If you try and log into a drive which is not currently physically in your system, i.e., you try to reference drive D: in a two drive system, CP/M will go off into never-never land and you will have to cold boot your system to get it to snap out of it.

CP/M has five built-in or resident commands (as opposed to transient commands which are loaded in from the disk and then executed). The resident commands are

DIR	Returns a directory of the current disk
ERA	Erases a file from a disk
REN	Renames a file
TYPE	Types out the contents of a file to the current console device such as the crt
SAVE	Saves the contents of memory as a file on the disk

We will now explain each of these special and often used resident commands.

DIR

Perhaps the command you'll use more often than any other is DIR. The DIR or DIRECTORY command allows the user to interrogate the disk to determine what files are on that disk. With DIR the user can either ask for a specific file, a group of files (using an unambiguous filename), or simply a general directory of a disk. The DIR function also allows the user to access a disk other than the current one without changing "current" disk. This is done by either typing DIR B: or some other drive reference (C, D, etc.) or by typing DIR B:BOOK.TXT where an ambiguous or unambiguous filename is preceded by a disk designation. CP/M version 1.4 and earlier will return the directory as a line of filenames, with each filename preceded by its drive designation. In versions 2.0 and later, the directory will be laid out in four columns.

If the user were to type, for example

```
A>DIR B:*.COM

B:STAT.COM
B:PIP.COM
B:ED.COM
B:ASM.COM
B:DDT.COM
B:LOAD.COM
B:DUMP.COM
B:MOVCPM.COM
B:SYSGEN.COM

A>[]
```

CP/M would return all of the files with a file type of .COM on disk B. Recall "*" is a wild card.

TYPE

The TYPE command will type out the contents of a file to the console device (usually the crt). This is usually the best way to quickly examine a file. The file must be a text file (i.e., it must contain ASCII characters) and it must have an unambiguous filename. The reason that the file must be a text file (such as .BAS, .FOR) is that object code files (files with file types of .COM, .REL, .CRF, etc.) have characters in them which might be interpreted as control characters and will tend to make the screen go crazy. In addition, since object code is machine readable, it is usually not human readable. Text files, data files, and program source listings will be readable using the TYPE command. Some of the file types that can be typed are .BAS, .FOR, .ASM, .MAC, .PRN, .LST, etc. The following example illustrates how to invoke the TYPE command.

This example will list the program source code for a BASIC program called GENLEDG.BAS to the console device. If a crt is being used as a console device, it is desirable to have the display pause as the screen will often scroll much faster than you can read. At any time, a CONTROL-S

```
A>TYPE GENLEDG.BAS

10 REM - - - THIS IS A PROGRAM TO
20 REM - - - BLAH DE BLAH
30 END

A>[]
```

can be typed to cause the display to freeze. Whenever another CONTROL-S is typed the display scrolling will resume. You may abort the listing of a file by typing any character other than a CONTROL-S while the listing is under way.

TYPE will not accept ambiguous filenames. Thus the following is an unacceptable use of TYPE. (In this case how would CP/M know what BASIC file you wanted typed?)

```
A>TYPE *.BAS
```

However, multiple files may be typed with one command. This is accomplished by separating each filename with a comma:

```
A>TYPE        LEDGER.BAS,MONTH.DAT,BOOK.TXT
```

ERA

The ERA or ERASE command is used to erase one or more files from the currently logged disk. The ERA command will accept both ambiguous and unambiguous filenames. Since ERA *.* is a valid command using an unambiguous filename and considering that this command will erase all files on the currently logged disk, CP/M will prompt the console with "ALL FILES (Y/N)?", and wait for a Y response before it proceeds with such a potentially destructive command. As a safety precaution it is always a good idea to precede the ERA command with a DIR command so that you are sure you are erasing the file from the correct disk. One of the most commonly made mistakes using ERA in a multidrive system is erasing the right file, but on the wrong drive!

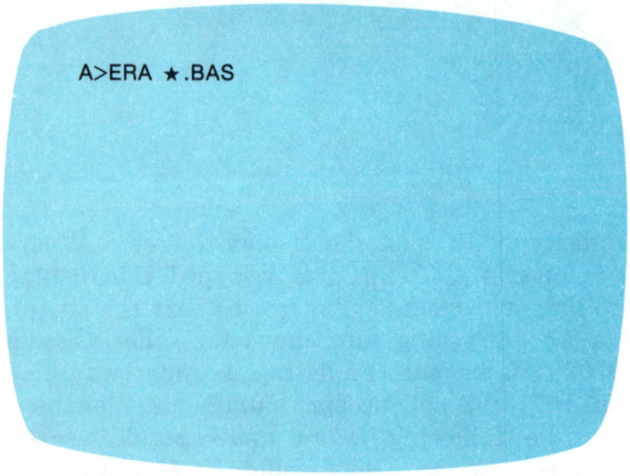

The preceding command will erase all BASIC source code files on the current disk.

REN

The REN or RENAME function allows you to change the name of a file from one name to another, while leaving the file itself intact. Renaming has many useful applications. The general form is as follows

The above command renames TEXT.TXT to TEXT.BAK. It is important to remember that the *new name comes first,* followed by the old name. If a file of the new name already exists, CP/M will abort the operation and print "FILE EXISTS" on the console. If CP/M can't find a file on the current drive with the old name then it will print "NOT FOUND" on the console. The *new name* may be preceded by a drive reference if you want to rename a file not on the current disk. The command for this would be

```
A>REN        B:TEXT.BAK=TEXT.TXT
```

To avoid confusion, CP/M will not accept ambiguous filenames in the REN function.

SAVE

SAVE is the final CCP resident command. SAVE is used mainly by those involved in assembly language programming, thus we will discuss SAVE only briefly here. A much more in-depth discussion can be found in the chapter on ASM and DDT. SAVE places n pages (256 byte blocks) into a file on a disk from the TPA. The following command will save the first 5 pages of memory (locations 100H through 4FFH) in the file PROGRAM.COM.

TRANSIENT COMMANDS (UTILITIES)

The most convenient CP/M commands to use are the five CCP commands which we just explained because they are built into the operating system. They are always there, and are quick to respond because you don't have to wait for them to be read in from the disk. However, they take up space, and can only do so much. Therefore, some of the more lengthy CP/M utilities must be stored on disk and called in when they are needed.

These programs are usually called utilities, in order to differentiate them from the resident commands. They must have a file type .COM, and are written to be loaded into memory starting at location 256 (0100H). CP/M has several standard utilities which are supplied with the system. They are

⊗ TRANSIENT COMMANDS

STAT.COM	ED.COM	DDT.COM
ASM.COM	PIP.COM	LOAD.COM
DUMP.COM	SYSGEN.COM	MOVCPM.COM

We will cover each of these utilities in much more depth in later chapters in addition to some other utilities which are not a part of the stock CP/M set of programs, and which are usually supplied by the various microcomputer manufacturers.

The general form to invoke a utility is to simply type the name of the utility. Notice, however, that only the filename, and not the .COM file type is entered. The following will invoke the STAT utility.

Utilities, like the resident commands, usually request some brief instructions as to exactly what function you would like to have performed. CP/M has the ability to pass these instructions along to the utilities, or if you wish, the utility will specifically ask you questions if no instructions are given when the utility is invoked. In order to pass commands on to the utility, simply type the command after the name of the utility, and before you hit the carriage return. The following will pass the command "*.COM" on to the STAT utility, load STAT into memory, and execute the command

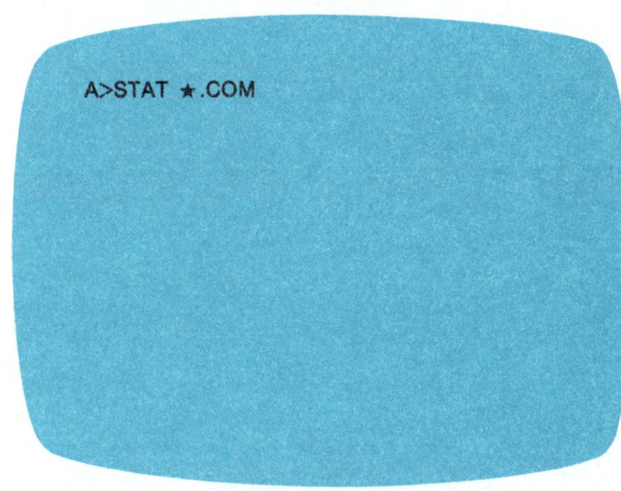

We will cover each of the standard CP/M utilities in detail in the following chapters. However, these nine utilities are not the only ones available. Many programmers have written utilities which perform such necessary functions as formatting an unused diskette, listing an ASCII file to the list device, and other functions too numerous to go into here.

A list of these programs as well as information on how to join the CP/M User's Group may be obtained by writing the CP/M User's Group (CMUG) at 164 West 83rd Street, New York, NY 10024. Once you are a member you will have access to all of the programs contained in the

CP/M User's Group Library for basically the cost of the diskettes which the programs are distributed on. If you plan to do any programming, you should consult CMUG first to make sure that the program you are interested in does not exist already in the Library. There is no sense re-inventing the wheel, unless you want to write a program as a learning exercise, or you just plain enjoy programming.

Appendix B contains a list of vendors who have written programs for the CP/M system, and a brief description of their programs. Most of these programs are not what is usually referred to as a utility; they are more high-level languages, or application programs. However, some of them should be classified as utilities, and will make the CP/M system on which they are run that much more useful and versatile.

chapter 4

System Initialization: FORMAT, SYSGEN, and MOVCPM

In Chapter 3 we talked about the various components of the CP/M operating system. We saw how the various modules, the CCP, BDOS, and BIOS interact, and the purpose for each of these components. In this chapter, we will look at the way in which CP/M can be modified and custom fitted to almost any microcomputer using an 8080, 8085, or Z80 microprocessor as the CPU.

HOW INFORMATION IS STORED ON A DISKETTE

The very first thing you will probably do when you use CP/M is initialize a blank diskette so that you can use it to store data, programs, text, and most importantly make "backup" copies of your CP/M disk. Most new diskettes come from the manufacturer initialized in some manner. However, it is always a good idea to reinitialize a diskette before you try and use it since your diskette may have been subjected to magnetic fields, x-rayed, or otherwise put in an environment that could erase some of the information on the diskette during transit.

For those of you who are not familiar with the way information is stored on a diskette, the following discussion should help. For those of you who are, you may skip this section and go on to Formatting a Blank Diskette.

Information is stored on a diskette in blocks of 128, 256, or 1024 bytes. Each of these blocks is referred to as a "sector." Each sector has a unique address or location on the diskette, and information is stored and retrieved by telling the disk controller to read or write information in a specific sector. The sectors are laid out on the diskette in concentric, circular tracks, with a specified number of sectors per track, as shown in Fig. 4-1. For example, an 8″ diskette *usually* has 26 128-byte sectors per track, and 77 tracks on each side of a diskette. Thus we would instruct the disk controller to *write* a block of information to Track 44, Sector 23; the controller would position the read/write head to Track 44, wait for Sector 23 to come around, and then it would write the information into that sector. The information could then be later retrieved by issuing a command to the controller to *read* Track 44, Sector 23.

Variations In Track/Sector Arrangement

As we hinted in the previous section, there are three formats for storing data on a diskette in common usage in microcomputers. The most common is the one we mentioned earlier called the "IBM 3470" configuration which is 128 bytes per sector and 26 sectors per track. This configuration uses a data recording method called single density (cleverly entitled since it stores one half the information per diskette as the other commonly used data recording method called, oddly enough, double density). Your computer may have the capability to record diskettes in double density, and you may wish to format your diskettes to a double density format prior to use. The two commonly used double density formats are 256 bytes per sector and 26 sectors per track, or 1024 bytes per sector and 8 sectors per track. With the double density formats, you can store a considerable amount of information on each diskette. For example, with a single density, 8″ diskette, you could get 256,256 bytes of storage on one side, but that number becomes 512,512 in double density using 256 byte sectors, and 633,248 using 1024 byte sectors. Recently, many manufacturers

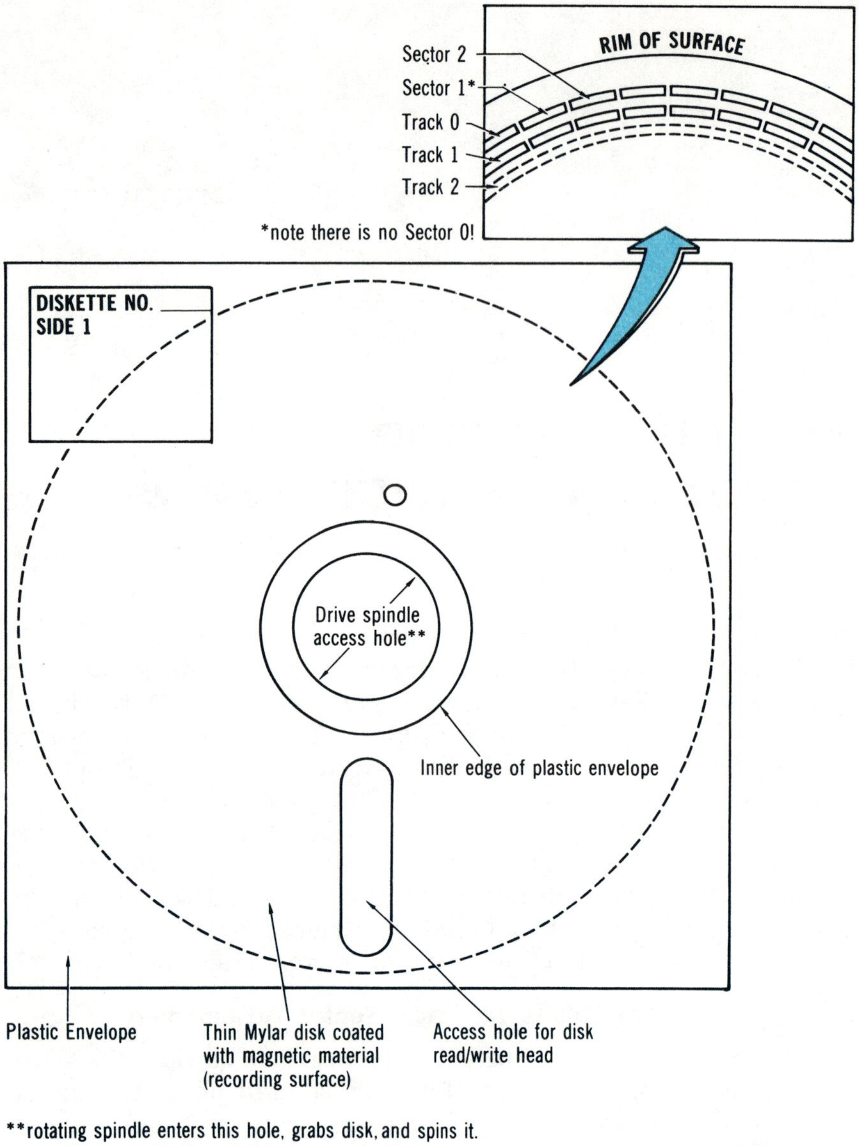

Fig. 4-1. Diskette track/sector layout.

have been selling double-sided disk drives. These allow you, as the name implies, to write on both sides of the diskette. If your computer is equipped with these drives, then you will be able to write on both sides of a double-sided diskette (yes, they are different, so watch out), and store twice the number of bytes listed above on a diskette.

Formatting a Blank Diskette

Formatting a diskette accomplishes two purposes in most systems, purposes which are vital to the error-free operation of your computer. The first is that the diskette must be set to the "blank" state (CP/M uses the byte E5H to denote "blank" sectors instead of 00H or FFH as one would assume). The second is that it will allow you to change the particular format of a diskette from one format to another. Thus if you would like to change a diskette from single to double density so that you can store more information on it, then you must reformat it before you try to use it in its new capacity.

Most manufacturers supply some sort of utility to perform this initialization function. It is usually a program called FORMAT.COM. However, since this is not a utility supplied by Digital Research as part of the stock CP/M set of programs, it may be called something else by the manufacturer. In order to run most FORMAT programs, you place a diskette with the FORMAT utility in drive A:, and place the diskette which you want to initialize in drive B:. Then you simply type the following command.

```
A>FORMAT
```

The FORMAT program will then typically ask you a number of questions about the way in which you would like your diskette formatted (single or

FORMAT

double density, 128, 256, or 1024 bytes per sector, etc.). After you answer these questions, the program will then format the diskette per your wishes, and then exit to the CP/M CCP.

At this point you can use the diskette to store data, programs, and text. However, since it does not have the CP/M operating system on it, it must be used with another diskette containing the system. A diskette like this with no system on it is called a "Files Only" diskette, as opposed to a "System" diskette which contains not only data, program, and text files, but a copy of the CP/M operating system. In a typical application, drive A: must have a "System" diskette in it, and the other drives in the system (B:, C:, etc.) can have either a "System" diskette or a "Files Only" diskette.

COPYING A CP/M SYSTEM

When you are creating a System diskette, you will want to either copy the CP/M operating system as it is to the new diskette, or you will want to modify it in some way first, before you copy it. For example, you might have a 32K CP/M system. You could either copy this 32K system to your new diskette as is, or you could make it into a 48K system first, and then copy it. Remember, however, when you are making this new system that the size of the system can always be less than the actual amount of memory you have in your computer, but never more. Thus, while a 32K CP/M system will run fine in a computer with 48K of memory, a 64K CP/M system will not run at all in that computer.

If you want to copy a system "image" (image is a word often used in the computer industry to describe an operating system program, which we will use here since it lends itself very nicely to allegory when we talk of copying and duplicating the operating system), then you will use the SYSGEN utility. For those situations where you want to change the system image, the MOVCPM utility will be used.

In order to copy the CP/M system image from the diskette drive A: to drive B: you would perform the following steps. First, place a diskette with the CP/M system image, and the SYSMOV, MOVCPM, and FORMAT utilities on it in drive A:. Then, place a blank diskette (or diskette which you don't mind erasing, since the following steps will erase all information previously stored on the diskette) in drive B:. The following commands will then format the diskette, and make an identical copy of the CP/M system image on the diskette in drive B:.

```
A>FORMAT B:
FORMATTING COMPLETE
A>SYSGEN
SOURCE DRIVE NAME:A
DESTINATION DRIVE NAME:B
DESTINATION ON B, THEN TYPE RETURN
DESTINATION DRIVE NAME:
A>
```

The first line invokes the FORMAT utility to initialize the diskette. We will assume here, for the sake of argument, that the command

MOV CP/M

```
FORMAT B:
```

will format the diskette in drive B: in the same way that the diskette in drive A: is formatted (i.e., same number of bytes per sector and sectors per track). The FORMAT utility will respond with the message

```
FORMATTING COMPLETE
```

when the entire diskette has been formatted.

The next line in our example invokes SYSGEN, the CP/M utility which we will use to copy the system image from diskette A: to diskette B:. You can answer the question of "which drive to take the system image off of" (SOURCE DRIVE NAME:) with the name of any drive which contains a diskette with the CP/M system image on it. SYSGEN will then ask you what drive to move the system to (DESTINATION DRIVE NAME:). You can answer with any drive in your system with a diskette in it, whether it has a system image on it already or not.

Once you tell SYSGEN which drive to copy the system image to, it will respond with a message to tell you which drive to put the system on so that you can check yourself that you have not inadvertently typed in the wrong drive name. When you type a carriage return SYSGEN will then copy the system image from the source diskette to the destination diskette. In order to allow you to initialize a number of diskettes at one time, as you will probably want to do, SYSGEN will continue to prompt you with the question

```
DESTINATION DRIVE NAME:
```

until you answer with a carriage return, which will terminate the SYSGEN utility and return you to the CCP. This allows you to move the system image to any number of diskettes, without having to recall the SYSGEN utility each time you move CP/M to another diskette.

MODIFYING A CP/M SYSTEM IMAGE

Often times it is necessary to change the CP/M system image to fit different amounts of memory. (Note that this is different than changing the BIOS module for a different hardware configuration. We are simply changing the amount of memory that the CP/M system image *runs* in, not the system image itself.) This can happen when you first get your CP/M system (which is usually a 16K system) and you need to configure it for the actual amount of memory in your computer, or later on, when you acquire more memory, or need to create a CP/M system image that does not use all of your computer's memory for one reason or another. The MOVCPM utilty is provided for this purpose.

The MOVCPM utility allows you to create a system image for any memory size. It is invoked with the following command

```
A>MOVCPM n *
```

where n is the optional memory size (in K bytes), and * is an indicator that the new system image should be preserved in memory for transfer to a diskette with the SYSGEN utility. If n is omitted, then MOVCPM will examine your computer's memory, starting at memory location 0100H and find the highest available memory location. It will then create a system image to match that amount of memory that it determines exists.

If the current system image is for a 16K system and we wanted to create a 32K system, and place the new system image on disk B:, then you would type the following commands.

```
A>MOVCPM 32 ★
READY FOR "SYSGEN" OR
"SAVE 32 CPM32.COM"
A>SYSGEN
SOURCE DRIVE NAME:
DESTINATION DRIVE NAME:B
DESTINATION DRIVE NAME:
A>
```

This set of commands will modify the current 16K system image in memory to a 32K system image. The "*" tells MOVCPM to leave the new system image in memory so that the SYSMOV utility can be invoked to move it to drive B:.

TRYING OUT YOUR NEW CP/M DISKETTES

Once you have followed the steps outlined above, you will have one or more diskettes with a CP/M system on them. You should be able to take them, place them one by one into drive A:, hit the RESET button on your computer, and have the CCP prompt

```
A>
```

appear on the screen. If any of your diskettes do not do this, then they should be reinitialized. If you still cannot get a diskette to boot, but you have been able to initialize other diskettes which boot, then you most likely have a bad diskette, and should not use it.

At this point, the new diskettes have no data, programs, or text on them, except the CP/M system image which we placed there with the SYSGEN utility. In the next chapter we will describe the PIP utility, which will allow us to transfer files from other diskettes onto our newly initialized diskettes on a file by file basis.

Many manufacturers have programs which make exact duplicates of diskettes, i.e., make a mirror image of the diskette in drive A: on the diskette in drive B:. They are usually called DISKCOPY or some name similar to that. These programs accomplish the same function as SYSGEN and PIP together in that they copy both the system image as well as all of the files from one diskette to another.

chapter **5**

STAT and PIP

STAT (Status) and PIP (Peripheral Interchange Program) are probably the most commonly used of the CP/M utility programs (or transient commands). Recall that we call these "transient" commands because they are .COM type files and are executed when their name is typed. They are used along with the resident commands to do all system "housekeeping" and file transfers. All operating systems have a similar function to STAT and PIP, although they may have a different name. Moving programs and files about the storage media is a job that must be performed often in the operating system. Determining the size of a file is equally important so we can tell whether the file to be moved will fit where we want it to go. PIP and STAT are used extensively when making backup diskettes or copying programs from one disk to another. We therefore suggest that you pay particular attention to this section.

STAT

STAT OVERVIEW

STAT is the transient command which allows the user to determine the condition or *STAT*us of CP/M files, such as the size of files. It is a very flexible program which allows the interrogation of disks, files, i/o devices, and other system functions. In order to use STAT, you must have the file STAT.COM on one of the disks in your system. In order to check this, type

```
A>DIR STAT.COM

STAT.COM
```

As we learned earlier, if STAT.COM is present, the CP/M system will return as indicated above. If STAT.COM is not on that particular drive, CP/M will respond as shown below. This means that the file STAT.COM is not currently present on drive A. Not to worry . . . yet. You probably have more than one drive in your system, so set the current drive to B, and then C, and so on until you find STAT.COM (this is described in detail in Chapter 3).

```
A>DIR STAT.COM

NOT FOUND
```

If after all this searching you still haven't found STAT.COM, then you must find a diskette with STAT.COM on it and put it in drive A. Once found you are set to explore your system with the aid of STAT. We illustrated this scenario because it is one that happens frequently in using an operating system—finding the disk with the particular program you're in need of—and we suggest you keep a catalog of what disks contain what programs just to be safe.

STAT AND DISK FILES

STAT can provide you with all kinds of information about the number, size, and kind of files on any given disk. (In some respects, STAT is like a sophisticated version of the DIR command.) It can also tell you how much room remains for files on the disk (very important, as you will no doubt soon find out that diskettes are far from limitless in their size!).

STAT, like all transient commands, can accept and interpret a command line. The command line is typed in immediately after the name of the transient program, and contains all input up to the carriage return.

STAT will recognize five disk-related requests in the command line. They are listed in Table 5-1, along with their functions.

Table 5-1. Five Disk-Related Requests and Their Functions

STAT	If the user types in an empty (plain vanilla) command line (i.e., typing STAT followed by hitting the CR key), STAT will simply display the amount of unused storage available on the currently logged-on drive.
STAT x:	A variation of the empty command line is to include a drive designation. STAT will return the amount of unused storage on drive x.
STAT ufn	STAT can also tell the user specific information about a file. By typing an unambiguous file name in the command line (ufn), STAT will return information about the size of a file in both bytes and records.
STAT afn	A variation of the preceding command which allows the information on a group of files to be displayed at a single time. The afn means, for example, ★.COM which list all of the .COM type files.
STAT x: = R/O	This command line allows the user to define an entire disk as read-only. Be sure and note that this restriction can only be removed by rebooting the system (either a warm or a cold boot).

In order to see exactly how each of the five disk-related command lines works, we will present some examples.

```
A>STAT A:

   BYTES REMAINING ON A: 185K
```

The first example asks CP/M to tell us through STAT how much usable space is left on drive A:. CP/M returns with a message telling us that there are currently 185K bytes of unallocated disk space left at our disposal. The second example gives a little more information; it shows the vital statistics for all of the files currently contained on drive B:. RECS is the number of records in each file, BYTS is the total file size in Kbytes, EX is the number of extents the file contains, and D:FILENAME.TYP is the drive, filename, and file type of the file. For an in-depth discussion of what an extent is, please refer to Appendix A: For now you can consider the extents a file has as being the major sections it is subdivided into. For example, a 50K byte file is spread across 4 extents. If you have more files on the disk than there are lines on your console device, then the list will simply scroll off the screen. If this happens, you can temporarily stop it by typing a CONTROL-S. To restart the listing, type a second CONTROL-S.

The final disk-related STAT command has to do with the ability to define a drive as read-only.

```
A>STAT B:*.*

RECS  BYTS   EX   D:FILENAME.TYP
 75    36K    3   B:ASM.COM
 50    25K    2   B:DDT.COM
 30    14K    1   B:ED.COM
  5     1K    1   B:LOAD.COM
 13     8K    1   B:PIP.COM
 25    12K    1   B:STAT.COM

 BYTES REMAINING ON B: 185K
```

This is accomplished with the R/O command. Once a drive has been marked as R/O, all subsequent attempts to write to the drive will generate an error message, and will cause CP/M to warm boot, as it always does when an operating system error is encountered. This feature can be very beneficial in situations where valuable information is contained on a disk, and the user wants to ensure that it is not accidentally modified or erased. By simply STATing the drive to R/O, the files on that drive are protected from being renamed, modified, or erased. The R/O command can be thought of as "locking" the disk so it can't be written to.

```
A>STAT B:=R/O
```

I/O DEVICES AND STAT: SPECIALIZED USES

STAT also allows the user to control the logical to physical device assignments, as well as the disk-related functions we just described. As we mentioned in Chapter 2, CP/M allows the use of logical device names to be assigned to actual physical i/o devices so that CP/M programs may be run on a large number of microcomputers.

To recap, CP/M provides the user with four logical device names that can be assigned to any number of physical i/o devices. In practice, only two of the logical devices get much use, the CONSOLE device and the LIST device. (Recall, the READER device and the PUNCH device are very seldom used and so we will spend most of our time dealing with the CON: and LST: devices.)

The actual physical i/o devices all need some kind of program to run them. These programs, or "driver" subroutines as they are usually called, are contained in BIOS. Once the subroutines have been included in BIOS to allow a number of i/o devices to be used with CP/M, these physical i/o devices may be switched around from logical device to logical device. For instance, if you had a crt terminal driver, a high speed line printer driver, and a modem driver installed in BIOS, you could set the logical CON: device to be either the modem or the terminal, and the LST: device could be any one of the three.

CP/M has standard names assigned to several "dummy" physical i/o devices. These names and their corresponding meanings are listed below. Remember, however, that just because a driver is assigned the name Line Printer, that does not mean that it must actually drive a line printer. It may actually drive a modem. The only restriction is that the device must have the same i/o characteristics as the "dummy" device would. In other words, you would not place the driver for an output-only device like a printer in a "dummy" physical i/o device which had input capability such as a crt terminal. The point is, the drivers in BIOS control what is actually driven by the device names.

TTY:	Teletype device (slow speed console)
CRT:	Crt device (high speed console)
BAT:	Batch processing
UC1:	User defined console
PTR:	Paper tape reader
UR1:	User defined reader #1
UR2:	User defined reader #2
PTP:	Paper tape punch
UP1:	User defined punch #1
UP2:	User defined punch #2
LPT:	Line printer
UL1:	User-defined list device

In case all of this is a little too much to remember, CP/M will come to your aid to remind you if you ask it to. STAT will print all of the possible logical to physical assignments possible by simply typing STAT VAL: as shown below.

This tells us, for instance, that the CONSOLE device can be one of the devices assigned to the TTY:, CRT:, BAT:, or UC1: drivers, but that it can't be the line printer device (LPT:).

```
A>STAT VAL:

  CON:=TTY: CRT: BAT: UC1:
  RDR:=TTY: PTR: UR1: UR2:
  PUN:=TTY: PTP: UP1: UP2:
  LST: =TTY: CRT: LPT: UL1:
```

The user may change any and all of the current assignments by simply typing a command line where the left side of the equals sign is one of the four logical devices, and the right side is one of the "dummy" physical i/o device drivers. For example, STAT CON:=CRT: will assign the CONSOLE device to the CRT screen and keyboard. Thus to display the current i/o assignment, change one, and then redisplay the assignments, the following sequence would be typed.

```
A>STAT DEV:

  CON:=CRT:
  RDR:=TTY:
  PUN:=TTY:
  LST: =TTY:

A>STAT LST:=LPT:

A>STAT DEV:

  CON:=CRT:
  RDR:=TTY:
  PUN:=TTY:
  LST: =LPT:
```

That's all for STAT for now. You'll probably find STAT will be used over and over in your work with CP/M.

PIP OVERVIEW

PIP (Peripheral Interchange Program) is the CP/M transient command used to move a file from one disk to another, and to make copies of files. PIP is one of the more often used CP/M transients, and it can do many important things such as outputting a file to a logical device such as a list device. Since 99% of the time PIP is used to transfer files from disk to disk, we will leave it to the reader to consult the CP/M manual "An Introduction to CP/M Features and Facilities" for details on the more esoteric PIP capabilities; here we will stick with the basics.

PIP can be invoked with or without a command line. If PIP is given a command line when it is invoked it will execute it and then return to the CCP and give you back the A> prompt. If no command line is input when PIP is first invoked, it will prompt the user (with its own prompt character "*" letting us know we are in PIP) for command lines continuously until a null command line is input (a null command line is when we sim-

ply type return in response to the PIP prompt). At that point PIP will return control to the CCP.

The general form of a PIP command line is

```
D:FILENAME.TYP=D:FILENAME.TYP
```

where the left side of the equals sign is the destination file and the right side is the source, and D: is an optional drive name. Thus the following will invoke PIP in the continuous command line form and transfer the file STAT.COM from disk A: to disk B:.

```
A>PIP

★B:STAT.COM=A:STAT.COM
★cr

A>
```

Note that the source file still exists on drive A:, we only *copied* it using PIP, not actually *moved* it. It is possible with PIP to eliminate the filename part of the destination in the command line if you are simply transferring a file from one disk to another and not renaming it. Thus the command line above could also be input

```
B:=A:STAT.COM
```

PIP will accept ambiguous filenames, so that you could transfer all .COM files from one disk to another by typing

```
B:=A:*.COM
```

OTHER PIP FEATURES

PIP will also let you rename an unambiguous filename during a transfer by simply changing the filename on the destination side of the equals sign to the new filename desired. If, for instance, we wanted to make a backup copy of this text on drive B:, we could input the following command line

```
B:CPMBOOK.BAK=A:CPMBOOK.TXT
```

Now the original filename is on A: with the name CPMBOOK.TXT, and the copy is on B: with the name CPMBOOK.BAK. Much of the time PIP is used to make such backup copies of files. To guarantee that the backup is copied perfectly, an option can be specified which will cause PIP to read back each file after it writes it, comparing the destination file with the source file, and report any errors detected. Ending a command line with a "V" enclosed in right and left square brackets will invoke this option. Note that this is not a toggle; the [V] must be typed at the end of every command line where verification is desired.

The sample session on page 44 shows a number of valid PIP command lines in the continuous command line mode.

The first line B:=A:*.COM[V] copies all .COM type files from the A: drive to the B: drive and verifies the copy is error free. The second line copies the transient STAT from drive A: to drive B:, and then verifies the transfer. The final example copies all files with the file type .DAT from drive A: to drive B:. In the process it renames all of the files from file type .DAT to .BAK.

You may wish to spend time playing with PIP and STAT as soon as you get your CP/M system

```
A>PIP

★B:=A:★.COM[V]
★B:STAT.COM=A:STAT.COM[V]
★B:★.BAK=A:★.DAT
★cr

A>
```

running. Coupled with FORMAT (see Chapter 4), you'll be able to make innumerable copies of your disks.

chapter **6**

ED the CP/M Editor

Up to this point we have dealt specifically with CP/M features that manipulate and move about whole files, namely the resident commands (such as DIRectory, ERAse, etc.) and the utilities (STATus and PIP). But what about getting inside a file or creating our own files? Or what about examining and changing the contents of existing files?

Although there are several kinds of files (.COM, .BAS, .TXT) the kind we "get inside" the most is the text file. A text file is made up of characters: letters, numbers, and the common punctuation symbols. A file of characters is created with another special utility program called the "Editor" (oddly enough!). The Editor is like an electronic typewriter, but typing puts the characters in memory instead of on paper!

ED is the name of the particular editor that comes with the CP/M operating system. ED allows you to create and alter source files for submitting to the assembler (ASM, see Chapter 7), BASIC-E, and other languages that require a program to be entered into a file before it is executed. ED can be used to input, display, and/or alter any ASCII text file under CP/M given the file is in ED's expected format. In addition, it can be used to alter BASIC-E and other language data files, and the assembly listing files produced by ASM.

ED is a "line oriented" text editor (as opposed to a "screen oriented" text editor), and not a word processor in the usual sense. This is an important distinction, because if you ask ED to do many of the things that a word processor will do,

ED: THE CP/M EDITOR

you will be disappointed. A word processor will typically display text on the screen as it will appear on paper, including right and left justification, underlining, page numbers, headings and footings, and other sophisticated text enhancements. ED will not do any of these things, although it will provide all of the basic editing features necessary to create and alter text files (ED will display text files, find words and things like that, of course). Thus if you are planning on using your computer to do extensive word processing, you should purchase a word processing package from one of the dozen or so currently on the market for use on microcomputers running under the CP/M operating system. Enough said about word processors. Now, on to ED!

INITIATING ED

An ED session can be initiated by typing the CP/M console command shown below, where FILENAME.TYP is any unambiguous filename, optionally preceded by a drive name. The specified filename is the file that will be altered when ED "comes up." If the file does not exist on the disk, then ED will create a new, but empty file by that name and will do so by typing

```
NEW FILE
```

on the screen. ED will then store all text entered and edited during that session in the newly created file. When we say ED created a file what we mean is that CP/M now has a file allocated on the disk, and a name is located in the disk's directory that points to the file.

When ED is ready to accept a command, it will prompt you with the "*" prompt character as shown below. As with all CP/M utilities, ED commands and command lines are terminated with a carriage return.

ED OPERATION

The overall operation of ED is shown in Fig. 6-1. ED reads the disk source file FILE.TXT into a memory buffer. Text in the RAM based memory buffer may then be altered without disturbing the disk. Text which has been edited may be written into the temporary file under command of the operator at any time in the edit. Upon termination of the edit, the memory buffer, along with any unread text coming from the disk source file FILE.TXT is now read into the temporary file FILE.$$$. The original source file FILE.TXT is renamed to FILE.BAK and the temporary file FILE.$$$ is renamed as the new FILE.TXT. This allows the user to have access to not only the latest version of the text, but also the next to the last version. In the event that an error is made on the latest version (like you inadvertently commanded ED to destroy, without regard for your sanity, the last 250 lines of the text), you can reclaim the last good version using the ERAse and REName commands. You would type, for example, A>ERA SORT.FOR to erase the now ruined program, and then A>REN SORT.FOR=SORT.BAK to make the backup for our "new" version. You have *no* backup now so you would immediately do an ED E edit function just to be able to rewrite a new .BAK file.

The purpose of the RAM memory buffer and its associated commands is to allow not only the alteration of text, but also to allow a file which is larger than the amount of RAM memory in your microcomputer to be edited nonetheless. When you are working on a short file, the whole file can be read into the memory buffer at one time, and you can disregard thinking about the buffer mechanism. However, the actual exact number of lines which can be read into the memory buffer at one time depends on the number of characters in a line (length of the lines), and the amount of RAM memory you have in your computer. So if your text exceeds the buffer length, the disk would read and write additional lines into the buffer.

The two ED commands which are used to transfer text between the source and temporary files and the memory buffer, and that are used right away with ED, are the APPEND (A) and WRITE (W) commands. They are typed into the command line in the form nA to *read* or *append* the next n lines from the source file into the memory buffer, and nW to *write* the first n lines from the memory buffer into the temporary file. The WRITE command will automatically shift the

ED OPERATION

lines remaining in the memory buffer to the top of the buffer. In order to better understand this, imagine the top of the buffer is the top of the first page of a book and the bottom is the last page.

In both cases n represents any number between 1 and 65535. If a pound sign (#) is given in the place of n, then the value of n is assumed to be 65535 or "all" lines. This form of the command is

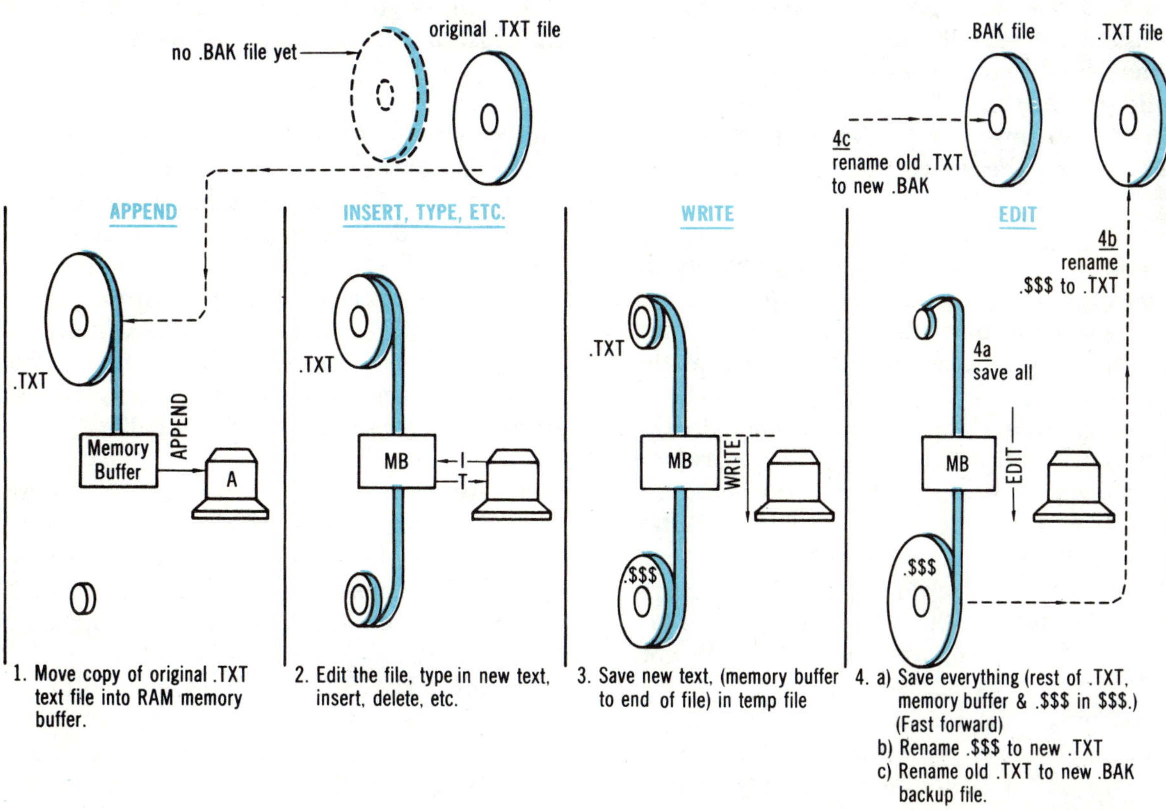

Fig. 6-1. How ED Defines files. A file here is analogous to a reel of film (with each frame a single character).

useful to append a file into the memory buffer or write a file to the temporary file from the memory buffer, when you are unsure of the actual file length, but know that it will fit entirely in the memory buffer. Thus, #A would append or read the entire file into memory, and #W would write the entire buffer contents to the temporary file. If you guess wrong and the buffer size is exceeded, then ED will issue you an error message, and you may then proceed with any ED command or function which does not increase the amount of text in the buffer (such as WRITING some of the text out of the buffer into the temporary file). If n is omitted, then ED assumes that n is 1. Thus, A and W append and write one line of text respectively.

In addition to the memory buffer, source file, and temporary file, ED has one more important component, called the character pointer. ED regards all text files as a series of lines of text, each separated by a carriage return. The operator can move the character pointer through the memory buffer on command. The character pointer (abbreviated CP here) is always located AHEAD of the first character of the first line, BEHIND the last character of the last line, or BETWEEN two characters. In other words, if you are about to edit a file, to say change a wrong letter you need to "move" the character pointer to the location of the bad character. The CP is the reference point for all edit commands, so it is important that you know where the CP is at all times while you are in an edit. The CP is always located inside the memory buffer and cannot be moved into either the source or temporary files.

Inserting Text

When you start ED, the memory buffer is empty. You may at this point either append lines from an existing file into the buffer, or you may enter new text. New text is entered using the insert or I command.

To initiate the insert mode you respond to the prompt by typing an "I" followed by a carriage return as shown at the top of the next column. This (typing I) is a pretty common way to enter text editors in general. As soon as you hit I and return, ED line feeds and does a carriage return as shown in the figure. The CP is now at the beginning of the buffer (or at the top of it if you like).

When you enter the insert mode, ED will accept all lines of text typed in, and will place them in the memory buffer in the order you type them, until you signal ED that you wish to stop inserting text by typing a CRTL-Z and you fall back to

the ED command mode. The CP remains positioned after the last character entered. While inserting text, the rubout key may be used to delete the last character typed (it will print the character as it deletes it so you know which character was deleted). Also, for those large mistakes, you can type CRTL-U to erase the entire line of input and then simply retype it. That's all there is to inserting—you simply type in the program or text or whatever and do a CRTL-Z when done to exit the insert mode. The ED prompt ("*") will then reappear.

Terminating an Edit

Assuming you are in the ED command mode, an ED session is normally ended with

```
E
```

This command writes the text in the RAM buffer to the temporary file, copies any remaining lines of the source file to this temporary work file, renames the files as previously described (source file to type BAK, work file to the same name and type as the source file), then initiates a system "warm boot" (remember, from Chapter 2), returning control to the Console Command Processor.

The following commands are also available for different ways to terminate an Edit:

- H Reedit: Move to head of new file and perform an automatic E command. Temporary file becomes the new source file, the memory buffer is emptied, and a new temporary file is created (equivalent to issuing an E command, followed by a reinvocation of ED using FILE.TXT as the file to edit). You use H when you want to update the .BAK backup file and return to the edit mode.
- O Original: Return to the original file. The memory buffer is emptied, the temporary file is deleted, and the pointer into the

source file is reset so that a subsequent A command will begin again at the beginning of that file. The effects of the previous editing commands are thus nullified.

Q Quit: Quit edit with NO file alterations, and return to CP/M.

Doing an H command often during an ED session is suggested, so that if the session is interrupted in any way, the state of the file as of the last H command will be on disk and less work will be lost. The H command is also used to start over when you wish to make an alteration in a part of the file you have already written out of the buffer.

Note that the Edit, H-Reedit, O-Original, and Q-Quit commands are not accepted in command strings.

BASIC EDITING COMMANDS

This is what an Editor is truly all about. And you'll eventually have to learn its particular set of commands. (Commit them to memory! To be proficient at juggling text around you must know them cold. However, once committed to memory, using the editor is like riding a bicycle!) Once there is some text in the buffer, various commands can be issued which manipulate the CP, display source text in the vicinity of the CP, or delete text. A summary of these commands is presented in Table 6-1. In the table, n represents a number from 0 to 65535. If n is omitted, 1 is assumed, as was the case of the Append and Write commands which we saw earlier. Similarly, "#" may be used in place of n and indicates 65535. +/− means a + or − sign; + is assumed if neither is given.

Any number of commands can be typed contiguously (up to the capacity of the CP/M console buffer which is 256 bytes long, which is roughly 3 lines on an 80 character screen), and are executed only after the carriage return is typed. The operator may use the CP/M console command editing commands Rubout and CRTL-U to delete a command or an entire line of commands.

```
ED LOAN.BAS
*#A
*4T
10 REM---PROGRAM BY MITCHELL WAITE
20 REM---WRITTEN: JULY 1978
30 REM---USED AS EXAMPLE IN THE BOOK BASIC
   PRIMER
40 REM---ALL RIGHTS RESERVED WORLDWIDE
*2L
*30C
*2D
*I
80^Z
*B
*4T
10 REM---PROGRAM BY MITCHELL WAITE
20 REM---WRITTEN: JULY 1980
30 REM---USED AS EXAMPLE IN THE BOOK BASIC
   PRIMER
40 REM---ALL RIGHTS RESERVED WORLDWIDE
*H
```

In order to get an idea of how a "line oriented" text editor like ED is used, we present the above example session. In this example we'll assume we have a BASIC program, and we wish to modify

Table 6-1. Summary of Basic Editing Commands

Means	Command	Description
Move to beginning bottom	+/−B	Move the CP to the /Bottom beginning of the memory buffer if +, and to bottom of the memory buffer if −.
Move through characters	+/−nC	Move CP by +/− characters (toward end of buffer if +), counting the carriage return/line-feed <cr> <lf> as two distinct characters.
Delete characters	+/−nD	Delete n characters ahead if +.
Kill lines	+/−nK	Kill (i.e., remove) +/−n lines of source text using the CP as the current reference. If the CP is not at the beginning of the current line when K is issued, then the characters BEFORE the CP remain if + is specified, while the characters AFTER the CP remain if − is given in the command.
Move through lines	+/−nL	If n=0, then move the CP to the beginning of the current line (if it is not already there). If n does not equal 0 then move the CP to the beginning of the line which is n lines down (if +) or up (if −). The CP will stop at the top or bottom of the memory buffer if too large a value of n is specified.
Type lines	+/−nT	If n=0 then type the contents of the current line up to the CP. If n=1 then type the contents of the current line from the CP to the end of the line. If n>1 and + is specified, then type the part of the current line after the CP along with n−1 lines which follow. Similarly, if n>1 and − is given, type the previous n lines, up to the CP. The rubout key can be depressed to abort long type-outs.
Move to line and type	+/−n	Equivalent to +/−nLT, which moves up or down n lines and types that line.

the program date text located at the beginning of the BASIC text file (some REM statements).

ADVANCED EDITING FEATURES

Text Search and Alteration

Here's where an Editor really shines . . . automatically searching for a word in your text. It is used when you have a special word used several places in text, and you wish to change all occurrences of it in some way. For example, suppose you have the word Model-8080 several times in a letter, and wish to change it to Model-6800. Or suppose in a program you want to change the variable called DELAY, which occurs on many lines, with a new name called TIMEDELAY. Well, quite nicely, Editors have the ability to "search" for a particular word, or text group, or character sequence. We call a character sequence a "string" in computerese.

ED has a command called Find which locates strings within the text memory buffer. The command takes the form

```
nF<Text>
```

where F means Find and <text> normally is the string you are looking for. You may terminate the text with a carriage return or a CTRL-Z. (You would use the CTRL-Z in cases where you were going to follow this command with one or more commands in the same command string, and did not want ED to be signaled that the command lines had been completely input with the carriage return.) ED scans forward through your text, starting at the CP, searching for the first occurrence of the desired text. If the text is found, the character pointer is positioned after the last character found in the string; if the text is not found the CP is not moved. The search will be repeated n times, and n will be evaluated to 1 if it is omitted. If the search fails, ED prints "##" and prompts for another command. If there were more commands in the string containing the F that failed, they are not executed.

As a convenience, a command similar to the F-Find command is provided by ED which automatically appends and writes lines as the search proceeds so you can follow the action. The form of N-Append and Write is

```
nN<Text>
```

where N means search for the nth occurrence of the text. The operation of the N command is precisely the same as the F command except in the case when the string cannot be found inside the current memory buffer. In this case, the entire memory contents is written back to disk (i.e., an automatic #W is issued). Input lines are then read from the file until the buffer is at least half full, or the entire source file is exhausted. The search then continues in this manner until the string has been found n times, or until the source file has been completely transferred to the temporary file.

An abbreviated form of the insert command is allowed, which is often used in conjunction with the F command to make simple textual changes. The form is

```
I <Text>
```

where <Text> is the string of characters to insert. If the insertion string is terminated by a CTRL-Z, the string inserted directly following the CP and the CP are moved directly after the inserted text. The action is the same if the command is followed by a carriage return except that a <cr> <lf> is automatically inserted into the text following the string . . . something you may or may not wish.

ED also provides a single command which, in effect, combines the F and I commands so you can find and substitute one block of text for another. The substitute command takes the form

```
nS<Old Text>CTRL-Z<New Text>
```

where S means Search and Replace, and <Old Text> and <New Text> are any strings of characters. The S command causes ED to search for the string <Old Text>, and, if found, delete it and insert <New Text> in its place. The CP is left after the last character of <New Text>. This operation is repeated n times; if n occurrences of <Old Text> are not found, ED will signal you by typing "##" and will await a new command input.

Source Libraries

Often, in programming, the user will wish to attach a preamble, heading, title, patent caution, copyright notice, or other text to a file being created. It could be horrendous to type this fixed data over and over each time it is used. Is there a way to store this special text in modules and add them to our program? No sweat with ED. We call them source libraries. However, there are no books in these libraries unless you write one. You use ED to create the file containing the often used text. You give it a .LIB extension.

ED allows you to include separate files from libraries into your text during the editing process with the R command. The form of this command is

```
R <Filename>
```

where R means Read and <Filename> is the name of a source file on the disk with an assumed file type of '.LIB'. ED reads the specified file, and places the characters into the memory buffer after the CP, in a manner similar to the I command. Thus, if the command

```
RTITLE
```

is issued by the operator, with the CP at the file beginning, ED reads from the file TITLE.LIB until the end of file, and automatically inserts the characters into the memory buffer. The CP will end up in front of the TITLE.LIB text in the buffer. You can build up many .LIB files quickly and place them on a special disk.

Repetitive Command Execution

The macro command M allows you to group ED commands together for repeated evaluation. The M command takes the form

```
nM <Command String>
```

where <Command String> represents a string of ED commands, but not including another M command. ED executes the command string n times if n>1. If n is omitted or n=0 or 1, the command string is executed repetitively until an error condition is encountered (e.g., the end of the memory buffer is reached with an F command).

If the command string ends in an I, S, etc. command, that command's string must be terminated with a CRTL-Z in addition to the carriage at the end of the line. For example the following inserts the line "REPEATED LINE" 10 times in a file, starting at the CP.

```
10MIREPEATED LINE ^L^Z<cr>
```

Upper and Lower Case

The Insert, Find, Search, N search for Nth commands convert letters in their <Text>s to upper case if the I, F, etc. is typed in upper case. If the command is typed in lower case (i, f, etc.), no such conversion will be performed.

The command

```
U
```

may be given to cause ED to convert all subsequent input to upper case. When U is in effect characters are echoed in the same case as typed, but go into the buffer in upper case. The command

```
—U
```

turns off this lower-to-upper case conversion.

ED ERROR CONDITIONS

In using an Editor you may frequently execute a command that leads to a type of failure, such as the inability to find the string you are searching for, or typing an unrecognized command. ED is not particularly rich in error messages, but it was not intended for use by nonprogrammers either or to be used as a word processor. On the following error conditions, ED types the indicator shown.

##	Search failure; The F, S, or N command cannot find given string.
??x	Unrecognized command character x. Also occurs if E, H, Q, or O is not the only command in the command line.
00	LIB file not found in R command.
>>	Memory buffer is full (Use any of the commands D, K, N, S, or W to remove characters) or F, N, or S string is too long.

If the memory buffer fills up during an Append command, >>A will be printed and the CP will be left at the end of the buffer (normally the CP is not moved by the A command). If the memory buffer fills up during an I command, >>x is printed, where x is the character that could not be inserted. In this case the CP is at the end of the inserted text.

If the diskette fills up, or its directory is full when ED needs to create or extend the work file, or some other file error is reported to ED by CP/M, ED prints

```
FILE ERROR
```

aborts, and returns to the CCP (A>).

If an edit is aborted for any reason (FILE ERROR, C (warm boot), Quit command, power failure, etc.), the source file is unchanged, the previous BAK file has been erased, and the temporary file (type $$$) is usually empty or incomplete.

Therefore, if an edit is complete, and later it is discovered that drastic errors were made, the original file (or its state as of the last H command, if any H's were used) can be reclaimed by ERAsing the new file and RENaming the BAK file to the original type. First, we recommend checking the contents of the BAK file, for example, with the CCP command

```
TYPE FILE.BAK
```

where x is the file being edited. Then remove the primary file

```
ERA FILE.TXT
```

and rename the BAK file

```
REN FILE.TXT=FILE.BAK
```

The file can then be re-edited.

ONE FINAL NOTE

There are many, many Editor programs out in the marketplace; almost every computer has at least *several* Editors available. CP/M is an extreme case, perhaps, but at last count over 33 text editor, text output formatter, and word processor programs were available! Someday you'll probably be faced with learning a new Editor's set of commands. Yes, they are all different, but there are many things done the same way. Usually it's just the keys chosen to do these things that change and cause the most problems. Any new Editor can be learned quickly if you hang a keyboard layout diagram next to the keyboard which explains the action of each key. The point is don't be afraid to learn many Editors. Between the authors, 7 different Editors have been used.

chapter 7

ASM: The CP/M Assembler

INTRODUCTION

In most cases, BASIC, FORTRAN, COBOL, and other high level languages are the best choice for programming an application. High level languages provide relatively simple Keywords for many programming routines. For example, all high level languages have some Keyword that will allow a procedure or set of steps to be performed some number of times. In BASIC, this looping is accomplished with the FOR...NEXT statement. This example prints out the numbers from 1 to 10

```
FOR I = 1 TO 10
PRINT I
NEXT I
```

In addition to providing simple commands for common procedures, high level languages have specialized data handling capabilities which allow different types of data to be manipulated easily. This data may be words, numbers, true/false conditions, etc. FORTRAN has excellent number handling features, such as various kinds of matrix operations, that make it well suited for number intensive applications, such as engineering and scientific research. COBOL, on the other hand, has a file structure that makes it best suited for business applications.

However, as with all things, high level languages are not always the best solution for all situations. There are applications which need some capability not found in the high level language being used. In these situations assembly language programs are often the solution. In many cases the assembly program is "attached" or hooked to the high level language. In other cases the entire solution is a program written in assembly language. Although in many respects programming in assembly language is more difficult than in a high level language, assembly language programming has several advantages over high level language programming that make it worth knowing.

All high level languages must convert a program from the syntax and structure of the high level language into the syntax and structure of the machine language of the CPU on which it is running. Thus, a BASIC interpreter must change the BASIC statements listed in the prior example into some set of machine language instructions. The number of machine language instructions needed to execute even this relatively simple section of a BASIC program could be quite large. To simply make the proper conversion from the BASIC language to a set of instructions which can be directly executed by the microcomputer will require a program consisting of several thousand statements or machine level instructions. Thus, the high level BASIC program will run more slowly than the same program written in machine language. So speed is another reason assembly language is chosen in some applications over high level languages.

ABOUT ASM, THE CP/M ASSEMBLER

An assembler is a utility which allows the programmer to create a program which is directly readable and executable by the microprocessor, without having to write the code in absolute machine language. ASM is an assembler capable of generating machine level code executable by 8080, 8085, and Z80 microprocessors.

What an Assembler Really Does

An assembler is like a converter that changes one thing to something that is identical in function, but different in its form. In computers, an assembler converts a sequence of "mnemonics"

THE CP/M ASSEMBLER

and "labels" created with the CP/M Editor, into a sequence of numbers. The numbers are what the microprocessor actually responds to; they are called object code or machine code. The mnemonics, in contrast, are called the assembly code. Assembly code is much easier for humans to work in than object code. Trying to understand what 00 EA 4C 60 00 is much harder than comprehending NOP LDA JMP 0060. The assembler does the conversion from mnemonics to object code.

To someone first becoming acquainted with assembly language programming, the seemingly endless lines of meaningless phrases can be tremendously confusing and intimidating. In order to help familiarize yourself with ASM while minimizing the amount of confusion, we will use a small assembly language program to illustrate some of the ASM features and features of assemblers in general.

The following program creates a pulse an exact number of milliseconds wide at the high order bit (bit 7) of port F0. This program is meant to be called from a BASIC program. The reason you would use this approach is because the BASIC program would not be able to time the start and stop of the time interval precisely enough. This particular program was written to run on an 8085 based microcomputer with a clock speed of 3 MHz. The clock speed is important for the timing loop (starting with the DCR B instruction and going through JNZ LOOP). A different clock speed on the microprocessor will require more or less NOP (No OPeration) instructions so that it takes exactly 1 ms to go through the loop. The BASIC program will use the POKE instruction (or some equivalent instruction that allows data to be placed directly in a RAM memory location) to transfer the number of milliseconds wide the pulse should be to the program. The calling program will POKE the number into memory loca-

8080 Architecture

In this chapter we will be discussing assembly language programming. This assumes that you know something about the microprocessor which you are going to be programming. We will digress here for a moment to try to give you an outline of the internal structure of the 8080. If you already understand the internal layout of the 8080 and its registers, then you can skip this section.

The 8080 has eight 8-bit registers and two 16-bit registers. Of the eight 8-bit registers, two of them are special purpose, but the other six may be paired off to form from one to three 16-bit registers. These 16-bit registers created this way are called "register pairs." Fig. 7-1 shows the 8080 registers.

PSW	ACCUMULATOR (8)	FLAGS (8)
BC	REGISTER B (8)	REGISTER C (8)
DE	REGISTER D (8)	REGISTER E (8)
HL	REGISTER H (8)	REGISTER L (8)
PC	PROGRAM COUNTER (16)	
SP	STACK POINTER (16)	

Fig. 7-1. Internal register set for 8080.

The letters to the side are the designators used to denote the 16-bit register pairs or registers. Data can be moved in and out any of these registers, with only a few restrictions. For example, the instruction MVI C,80H (Move Immediate to Register C) will load the C register with the value 80H. Likewise the instruction SHLD 0100H will store the 16-bit value from the register pair HL into memory locations 0100H and 0101H.

For a more detailed discussion of assembly language programming, we suggest that you read any one of the many books available on the subject.

tion D803 and then CALL location D800 to start the pulse.

The program is listed in Fig. 7-2. We will refer to various portions of it as we go along through the rest of our discussion on ASM. The program basically works like this. The program jumps over the ms count location in memory to the beginning of the main program. The registers are saved with the PUSH instructions. We want to first set bit 7 on the output port to 0. We do this by first clearing the accumulator and then outputting the contents of the accumulator to the port. We then get the ms count out of memory and store it in register C which we are going to use as the ms counter. We load the B register with the proper number of times which we need to go through the timing loop to get 1 ms. Once we have thus initialized everything, we are ready to start the count. We set bit 7 on the output port to 1 and then enter the timing loop. Every time we go though the loop, the count in register B is decremented, until it is zero which means that 1 ms has gone by. We then reset the B register with the loop count in case we have to do it again. We then decrement the ms count in register C, and loop again if another ms is required. If not, then we send a 0 to bit 7 of the output port, restore the registers with the POP instructions, and exit to the calling program.

```
           ORG      0D800H
OUTPORT:   EQU      0F0H
ON:        EQU      80H        ;TURN ON BIT 7
LTIME:     EQU      100D       ;LOOP COUNT=1 MS
           ;
ENTRY:     JMP      ENTRY+4    ;JUMP PAST COUNT
COUNT:     DB       0          ;INITIALIZE COUNT
           ;
MAIN:      PUSH H              ;SAVE REGISTERS
           PUSH D
           PUSH B
           PUSH PSW
           ;
           XRA      A          ;CLEAR ACCUM
           OUT      OUTPORT    ;SET BIT 7 to 0
           LDA      COUNT      ;GET MS COUNT
           MOV      C,A        ;SAVE IT
           MVI      B,LTIME    ;LOOP COUNT=1 MS
           MVI      A,ON       ;SET BIT 7 TO 1
           OUT      OUTPORT    ;START PERIOD
           ;
LOOP:      DCR      B          ;DECR LOOP COUNT
           NOP                 ;TIMER FILLER
           NOP
           NOP
           NOP
           JNZ      LOOP       ;LOOP IF MORE
           ;
           MVI      B,LTIME    ;RESET LOOP COUNT
           DCR      C          ;ONE LESS MS TO GO
           JNZ      LOOP       ;ONE MORE TIME!
           ;
           XRA      A          ;CLEAR ACCUM
           OUT      OUTPORT    ;END PERIOD
           ;
           POP      PSW        ;RESTORE REGISTERS
           POP      B
           POP      D
           POP      H
           ;
           RET                 ;RETURN TO BASIC
           END
```

Fig. 7-2. A sample 1 millisecond resolution timing loop.

In order to use ASM, you must first create a program source file such as the one above, with ED or some other editor. This file must have a file type of .ASM. You then can invoke ASM to convert this source file to object code by typing

```
ASM [D:]FILENAME
```

or

```
ASM [D:]FILENAME.PRM
```

where PRM is a list of parameters dealing with some input and output option supported by ASM which we will discuss in detail later in this chapter, and [D:] is an optional disk drive name where ASM can expect to find the assembly language source file.

ASM will then assemble the program and create two output files

```
FILENAME.HEX
```

and

```
FILENAME.PRN
```

(provided that the option to suppress the creation of these files has not been specified). The .HEX file contains the machine code corresponding to the original program in Intel hex format, and the .PRN file contains an annotated listing showing generated machine code, error flags, and source lines. The .PRN file can't be run since it is really a source file (i.e., human oriented text); it is a combination of not only the source code, but a hex listing of the machine code generated by ASM, as well as a list of all errors encountered by ASM. If errors are detected in the source code, they will be printed in the .PRN file as well as at the console during compilation.

As we mentioned above, ASM allows the user to pass arguments to it so that the input and output files of the assembler may be redirected somewhere besides the currently selected disk. This is done by appending a parameter word of up to three letters to the end of the FILENAME where the file type usually is. Remember, the file type of the input source file must always be .ASM; specifying parameters as a file type does not change the name of the input file that ASM looks for.

The parameters must be in the following form

FILENAME.xyz

where x, y, and z are single letters. ASM interprets these parameters in the following way.

x: A, B, etc. designates the logical disk drive name which contains the source file.

y: A, B, etc. designates the logical disk drive name which the hex file will be written to.

Z suppresses the generation of the hex file.

z: A, B, etc. designates the disk name which will receive the print file (listing).

X directs the listing to the console instead of in a file.

Z suppresses the generation of the print file (listing).

Thus, the command

ASM PROGRAM.ABX

indicates that the source file (PROGRAM.ASM) is to be taken from disk A, the hex file is to be placed on disk B, and the listing is to be sent to the console, instead of to a .PRN file. This is shown in the Fig. 7-3.

The command parameter .AZZ can be used to quickly assemble a program and check the syntax for errors (it is quicker because ASM does not have to write the .HEX or .PRN files to the disk). It will suppress the generation of both the hex file and listing file. Any errors will be listed on the console screen. In this particular example ASM would look for the input file on drive A, but the first letter of the parameter set could be any valid drive letter.

PROGRAM FORMAT

An assembly language program acceptable as input to the assembler consists of a sequence of statements of the form

LINE# LABEL OPERATION OPERAND ;COMMENT

such as

0031 LOOP DCR B ;DCR COUNT

where any or all of the fields may be present. The fields must be separated by one or more spaces or a tab character (CNTR-I), except that the operand field may contain imbedded blanks, but it must be terminated by a carriage return or semicolon (if a comment follows).

All lines must end with a carriage return or "!" after the last field in the line. ASM looks for one or the other of these characters to designate the end of the line, since not all of the fields need be present. The use of the "!" character in place of the carriage return allows multiple program statements per line, which can make the program easier to read and the listing shorter in some cases.

In the sample program we listed in Fig. 7-2 we used a series of POP and PUSH instructions to save the current contents of all machine registers

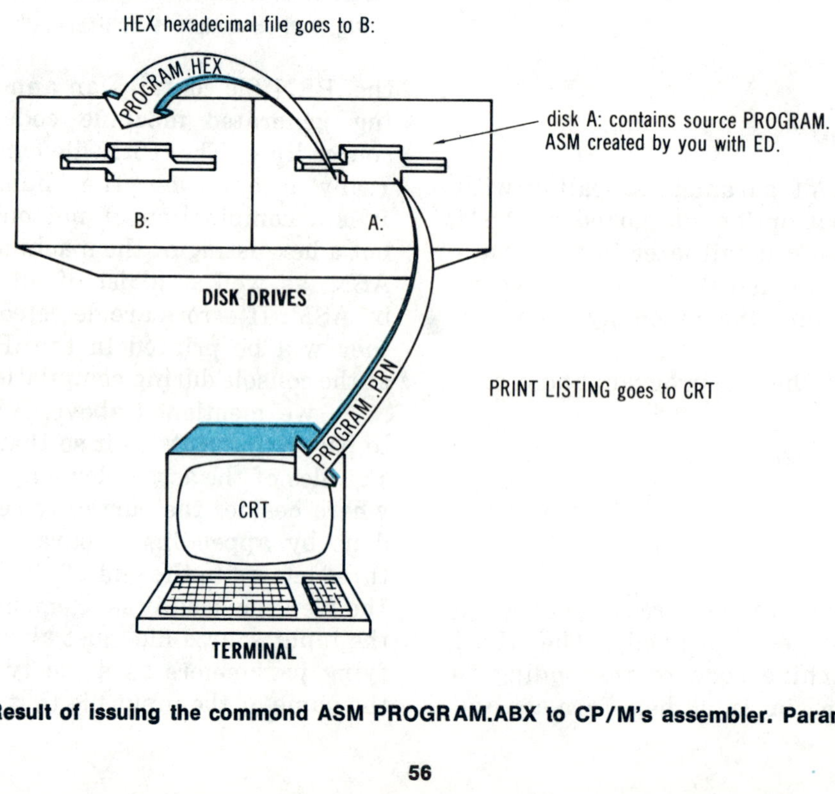

Fig. 7-3. Result of issuing the commond ASM PROGRAM.ABX to CP/M's assembler. Parameters are ABX.

upon entry into the program, and to restore them when we exited the program. Since this is standard programming practice, the program listing would be more readable if the PUSHes and POPs were all on one line. By using the "!" character we can do just that. The following two lines are directly equivalent to the four PUSH and four POP statement lines

```
PUSH H! PUSH D! PUSH B! PUSH PSW   ;SAVE REGS
POP PSW! POP B! POP D! POP H       ;RESTORE REGS
```

Line # can be any decimal integer. It is ignored by ASM, but the line number is permitted so as to allow programs created on line-oriented text editors which use numbers to be compiled by ASM. This is useful, for instance, if you have a program written with an editor other than ED that you would like to compile without completely rewriting the source code with ED.

The label is any sequence of alphanumeric characters up to 16 characters in length and beginning with an alpha character. It may or may not be followed by a colon, depending on the programmer's preference. In order to increase readability, you may imbed one or more "$" characters into the label. For example the label

```
JUMPTORESTART
```

is much more readable if it is broken up with "$" characters like this

```
JUMP$TO$RESTART
```

The "$" character is not significant to ASM, i.e., ASM will ignore all "$" characters and interpret the two examples listed above identically. The "$" character does not count as a character either when you are counting characters in reference to the 16 character label length limit.

The next field in the program line is the operation field. This field must contain a valid assembler directive (explained later in this chapter), pseudo operation, or 8080 machine operation code (mnemonic). The operation specified in the operation field often requires an operand to make any sense. The operand is placed in the next field, the operand field, and in general consists of expressions formed out of constants and labels, as well as any of the valid logical or arithmetic operators supported by ASM. For example,

```
EQU     0F0H
OUT     OUTPORT
MVI     B,LTIMER
```

are all valid operations that have operands.

The final field is the comment field. ASM interprets everything between the ";" and "!" or carriage return as a programmer comment. This field is always optional, and is ignored by ASM when it creates the object code. However, it is always good programming practice to liberally comment any program so that you and others may find it easier to read the program at a later date. This is particularly true of assembly language programming since it is far less structured than high level languages are, and hence any given statement could be performing almost any function in the program.

The actual assembly language program is simply a series of these program lines as described above in a specific order that, when translated from mnemonics into object code and executed by the computer, performs a desired function. The end of the program is designated by the end of the source code file or, optionally, an END statement. ASM will ignore any and all program statements in a source code file that come after an END statement.

Numeric Constants

A numeric constant is any 8- or 16-bit value used in the program. Due to the nature of machine language programming, ASM will recognize a numeric constant in any one of several bases (i.e., base 2, 8, 10, 16, etc.). We often find it more convenient to express constants in different bases, depending on their particular function in the program. For instance, addresses are best listed in hexadecimal, counters in decimal, etc. In order to indicate to ASM which base a constant is in, all constants should be followed by one of the following letters or indicators. ASM recognizes the following

B binary constant (base 2)
O octal constant (base 8)
Q octal constant (base 8)
D decimal constant (base 10)
H hexadecimal constant (base 16)

The reason that the octal constant has two indicators is that the character O is easily confused with the digit 0. ASM assumes that any constant that is not followed by an indicator is decimal.

The following are examples of valid constants in each base. Notice that as with labels, the "$" character is acceptable to use to increase readability, particularly with binary constants where it is used between the upper and lower nibble (a nibble is a 4-bit portion of an 8- or 16-bit value). Note also that all constants must begin with a digit. Since a valid hexadecimal constant may not always begin with a digit a leading 0 should be added if the first character is an alpha character so ASM will not interpret the constant as a label!

Binary (base 2):	11110000B
	1010$1000B
	1100$1010$0000$1101B
	1101101000110101B
Octal (base 8):	22670
	3325Q
	22$56$12Q
Decimal (base 10):	128
	48354D
	1234D
	1
Hexadecimal (base 16):	0FFH
	81H
	0DEF8H

String Constants

In addition to numeric constants, ASM will also recognize string constants. A string constant is any sequence of ASCII characters up to 64 characters long, which doesn't contain any ASCII control characters (any of the first 32 characters in the ASCII set). A string constant is represented by enclosing the string in apostrophe (single quote mark) characters. Unlike other characters in the source code file, ASM does not translate lower case letters enclosed in a string constant into upper case. If you want an apostrophe in the middle of a string constant, it may be represented as two successive apostrophes. Thus ASM will recognize this as an imbedded apostrophe and not the end of the string.

The following are valid examples of string constants.

```
'ERROR CODE 96'
'Please insert the diskette in drive A:'
'I said "Good Morning" to him.'
```

ARITHMETIC AND LOGICAL OPERATORS

As we mentioned earlier in this chapter, an operand may be made up of constants and/or logical or arithmetic operators. This allows for more efficient and easily readable programs to be written. Both arithmetic and logical operators may be used, and they may be mixed to form any mathematically valid expression. Table 7-1 gives a list of the operators recognized by ASM.

As you recall in our program, we have a data area in the middle of the program area. Thus we must interrupt the program code flow to go around the data area. We did this with the statement

Table 7-1. Operators Recognized by ASM

a + b	unsigned arithmetic sum of a and b
a − b	unsigned arithmetic difference between a and b
+ b	unary plus (produces b)
− b	unary minus (identical to 0 − b)
a ★ b	unsigned magnitude multiplication of a and b
a/b	unsigned magnitude division of a by b
a MOD b	remainder after a/b
NOT b	logical inverse of b (all 0's become 1's, 1's become 0's) where b is considered a 16-bit value
a AND b	bit-by-bit logical AND of a and b
a OR b	bit-by-bit logical OR of a and b
a XOR b	bit-by-bit logical EXCLUSIVE OR of a and b
a SHL b	the value which results from shifting a to the left by an amount b, with zero fill
a SHR b	the value which results from shifting a to the right by an amount b, with zero fill

```
JMP     ENTRY + 4 ;JUMP PAST COUNT
```

which uses the "+" or sum operator. ASM will evaluate this expression to 0D800H + 4 or 0D804H.

In order to avoid unexpected results, remember that ASM performs all operations with 16 bits, even if the operands are all 8 bits. Thus the expression

```
DDH + 0FH
```

will be evaluated to

```
00ECH
```

not

```
ECH
```

as would normally be expected by the uninitiated. Thus you could not load the sum of this operation into one of the 8-bit registers in the 8080. It would have to go into a register pair since it is 16 bits.

ASM assigns a relative importance to the operators listed above. They are broken into five levels, and in an expression with multiple operators the highest level operators are evaluated from left to right, then the second highest level from left to right, and so on. Of course, if you insert parentheses, ASM will interpret these first. The operators listed below on the same line have equal importance. All operators in each line have a higher precedence than the operators appearing on a lower line.

```
* / MOD SHL SHR
      - +
      NOT
      AND
     OR XOR
```

Thus the expression

```
a * b + c * d
```

will be evaluated as if the following parentheses had been inserted.

```
(a * b) + (c * d)
```

ASSEMBLER DIRECTIVES

ASM recognizes certain operations which are not in the 8080 instruction set and which are, indeed, not even machine instructions at all. These are referred to as "pseudo operations" and they can be used to direct ASM to set aside data storage areas, assemble or ignore certain sections of code, define variables, and set starting and ending address of the code produced by the assembler. The pseudo operations recognized by ASM are listed in Table 7-2.

Table 7-2. Pseudo Operations Recognized by ASM

ORG	Define starting address of the program or data section
END	End program assembly
EQU	Define a numeric constant
SET	Set a numeric value
IF	Begin conditional assembly
ENDIF	End of conditional assembly
DB	Define data byte
DW	Define data word
DS	Define data storage area

Pseudo operations are placed in the usual ASM operation field and may be preceded by a label and line number and succeeded by a comment in the line. All pseudo operations require an argument with the exception of the END and ENDIF directives. The arguments are placed in the operand field. The specifics of the directives are detailed below.

ORG:

The ORG (origin) directive sets the beginning absolute address of the program or a data section. It takes the form

```
label     ORG     expression     ;comment
```

where "label" and "comment" are an optional statement label and optional comment. "Expression" is a 16-bit value or expression which evaluates to a 16 value. (Remember, we are defining a memory address, so 8-bit values are not sufficient.) The ORG directive must come before the first statement to be assembled starting at the address defined by the ORG directive. A program may have several ORG statements if sections are to be assembled at different locations. Also be sure that if you use an expression instead of an absolute value for the "expression" portion of the directive, that the labels used in the "expression" have been defined in a prior statement. Most programs you will be assembling will be assembled to run in the CP/M TPA (Transient Program Area) which begins at memory location 0100H. Thus, these programs should have a statement

```
ORG     0100H
```

somewhere in the beginning of the program. ASM will assemble a program to begin at 0000H as a default if there is no ORG directive and a program assembled at that address will not run under CP/M as the memory from 0000H to 0100H is reserved for CP/M.

The program example, however, used a different origin (D800H). Because it must be run with a BASIC program, and the BASIC program is already assembled to run at memory location 0100H, we had to find somewhere else to put the object code. Thus the ORG statement

```
ORG     OD800H
```

END:

The END directive will stop assembly of a program at the line in which ASM encountered the END directive, whether or not there are more program lines in the input file or not. The END directive is optional; ASM will assume an END statement when it reaches the end of the input file. The END directive takes the form

```
label     END
```

EQU:

The EQU (equate) directive serves two purposes. It assigns a numeric value to a label so the label can be used throughout the program, and in doing so makes the program more readable, since labels are usually more explanatory than numeric constants as to their function. The form of the EQU directive is

```
label     EQU     expression
```

where "label" is the label to be defined, and "expression" is the expression that will be evaluated to define the label. It is considered good programming practice to define labels and use them instead of numeric constants throughout a program. For example, if you have decided to create a buffer starting at address 0D000H, you would do so with an EQU directive like the one below.

```
Buffer     EQU     0D000H
```

When you wish to reference it later in your program, say to load it into register pair H, you would do so with the following statement

```
LXI      H,Buffer
```

instead of

```
LXI      H,0D000H
```

which is a valid ASM statement, and would produce identical machine code. In addition to being easier to read, if you decided to move the buffer so that it started at memory location 0C800H instead, you would only have to change one line of the program if you used the EQU directive, instead of each line where the label is used. Once a label has been set with the EQU directive, it cannot be reset later in the program with another EQU directive. If you want to assign a value to a label, but want to change it later in the program, then use the SET directive explained below.

SET:

The SET directive is identical in form and operation to the EQU directive, except that a subsequent SET command can set the value of a label to a new value. Thus, while the value assigned by the EQU directive is good for the entire program, the value assigned by the SET directive is valid only until the next SET directive containing the label. The SET directive is used most often in controlling conditional assembly, explained below.

IF and ENDIF:

The IF and ENDIF directives allow you to include or exclude portions of a program during the assembly process. The form of the IF and ENDIF directives is

```
label     IF          expression
                      statement #1
                      statement #2
                      . . . . . .
                      statement #n
          ENDIF
```

ASM will evaluate the "expression" and if the value is logical true (nonzero, usually −1) then it will assemble statements #1 through #n. If on the other hand, the "expression" evaluates to a logical false (zero) value, then ASM will skip over statements #1 through #n, and resume assembly with the first valid statement after the ENDIF is encountered.

The IF and ENDIF directives are frequently used in the test and debugging stages of programming. For example, let us say you wanted to debug a program that contained a loop, and you wanted to know how many times the program went through the loop. The following program would do this

```
True      EQU      -1
False     EQU      0
Test      EQU      True      ;Test is on
;
          MVI      A,10      ;Times to loop
          MVI      B,0       ;Clear the B Reg
Loop:     DCR      A         ;One less loop to do
          IF       True      ;Start test routine
          INC      B         ;Increment test counter
          ENDIF
          JNZ      Loop      ;Loop back if more
```

At the end of the execution of this section of code, Reg B will contain the number of times the program went through the loop. Once the program has been debugged, the test section can be removed by simply changing the third EQU above to

```
Test      EQU      False     ;Test is off
```

However, it is still in the source code, and can be turned on by simply changing Test back to True at a later date.

DB, DW, and DS:

The DB, DW, and DS directives allow you to set aside and, in the case of DB and DW, initialize data storage sections. The DB directive initializes a series of successive memory locations with 8-bit values. The DW directive initializes a series of 16-bit values. The form of the directives is as follows

```
label     DB       v#1, v#2, ..., v#n
label     DW       v#1, v#2, ..., v#n
label     DS       expression
```

where "label" is an optional label, v#1 through v#n are 8-bit values in the DB directive, and 16-bit values in the DW directive. Note that the values in the DB directive can be a character string. For instance the directive

```
Emessage      DB      'You blew it!'
```

is valid and will store the error message for you. ASM will store each character in the string in a successive memory location. Also remember that the 8080, 8085, and Z80 microprocessors get 16-bit values from memory with the least significant byte stored in the lower address of the pair, and the most significant byte stored in the upper address of the pair. However, ASM already compensates for this so don't try and outthink it and reverse the order yourself; it will then be backward!

The DS directive evaluates the "expression" and reserves the number of bytes of memory specified by the value. The DS directive is used to reserve memory for use as data storage by the program,

```
A > ASM TIMER.AAX

ASM VERS 2.06

 D800                          ORG    0D800H
 00F0 =          OUTPORT:      EQU    0F0H
 0080 =          ON:           EQU    80H          ;TURN ON BIT 7
 0064 =          LTIME:        EQU    100D         ;MILLISECOND LOOP COUNT
                               ;
 D800 C304D8     ENTRY:        JMP    ENTRY + 4    ;JUMP PAST COUNT
 D803 00         COUNT:        DB     0            ;INITIALIZE COUNT
                               ;
 D804 E5         MAIN:         PUSH   H            ;SAVE REGISTERS
 D805 D5                       PUSH   D
 D806 C5                       PUSH   B
 D807 F5                       PUSH   PSW
                               ;
 D808 AF                       XRA    A            ;CLEAR ACCUMULATOR
 D809 D3F0                     OUT    OUTPORT      ;SET BIT 7 TO 0
 D80B 3A03D8                   LDA    COUNT        ;GET MS COUNT
 D80E 4F                       MOV    C,A          ;SAVE IT
 D80F 0664                     MVI    B,LTIME      ;LOOP COUNT FOR 1 MS
 D811 3E80                     MVI    A,ON         ;SET BIT 7 TO 1
 D813 D3F0                     OUT    OUTPORT      ;START PERIOD
                               ;
 D815 05         LOOP:         DCR    B            ;DECREMENT LOOP COUNT
 D816 00                       NOP                 ;TIMER FILLER
 D817 00                       NOP
 D818 00                       NOP
 D819 00                       NOP
 D81A C215D8                   JNZ    LOOP         ;LOOP IF MORE
                               ;
 D81D 0664                     MVI    B,LTIME      ;RESET LOOP COUNT 1MS
 D81F 0D                       DCR    C            ;ONE LESS MS TO GO
 D820 C215D8                   JNZ    LOOP         ;ONE MORE TIME!
                               ;
 D823 AF                       XRA    A            ;CLEAR ACCUMULATOR
 D824 D3F0                     OUT    OUTPORT      ;END PERIOD
                               ;
 D826 F1                       POP    PSW          ;RESTORE REGISTERS
 D827 C1                       POP    B
 D828 D1                       POP    D
 D829 E1                       POP    H
                               ;
 D82A C9                       RET                 ;RETURN TO BASIC PROG
                               ;
 D82B                          END                 ;END OF ASSEMBLY

D82B
000H USE FACTOR

A >
```

Fig. 7-4. Assembled PRN print listing of our sample timing loop program.

but which doesn't need to be initialized to any value. For instance the following directive will reserve 128 bytes of memory for a buffer to be used for disk i/o.

```
Dskbuff      DS      128      ;Reserve 128 bytes
```

A SAMPLE SESSION

The session shown in Fig. 7-4 will take the source program we listed earlier in this chapter and assemble it, placing the .HEX file on drive A: and directing the .PRN listing to the screen instead of as a file on the disk. Note that the source code and object code are included, along with the exact location addresses. Once ASM has assembled TIMER, it is set to be tested and debugged using the CP/M debugger DDT. We will cover the operation of DDT, as well as continue our sample sessions through the test and debug stages in the next chapter.

chapter 8

DDT: The CP/M Dynamic Debugging Tool

One of the things that makes assembly language programming so difficult is the debugging process. Software (programs) is defective by nature; that is to say almost all software has some kind of bug in it. Thus the ability to detect and correct errors in a program is critical in any programming, but due to the complexity of many assembly language programs, and the lack of structure inherent in most assembly language programming, it is much more important that assembly language programmers have capable and sophisticated debugging tools at their disposal. DDT is one such tool.

DDT (Dynamic Debugging Tool) has the ability to perform most of the tasks that an 8080 assembly language programmer would need to debug most 8080 assembly language programs. With DDT you can examine and modify memory locations and/or the actual CPU registers, assemble and disassemble binary machine language, and perform step-by-step tracing of program steps. In addition, it allows you to load and execute the hex file output from ASM.

THE PARTS OF DDT

DDT is comprised of two separate sections or modules. The first of these is the main nucleus of DDT itself. This is the section that interprets and executes all of the DDT commands, with the exception of the assemble/disassemble commands. The second section of DDT is the assembly/disassembly portion; we will say more about this later. The nucleus module is loaded in memory just below the EDOS CP/M module with the assembly/disassembly module right below it. When this is done the CCP is overwritten and lost. Thus, you must exit DDT by doing a warm boot to restore the CCP. This sequence is initiated by typing the command

```
A>DDT
```

DDT will respond as above with the sign-on message

```
nnK DDT VER x.x
```

where nn is the system size (same as the CP/M system you are currently running) and x.x is the revision number of DDT. DDT will then display the prompt "dash" character:

```
-
```

which lets you know that DDT is now in the command mode and is awaiting your every command.

Fig. 8-1 shows how the DDT nucleus is loaded into memory by the CCP when the command

```
A>DDT
```

is typed. Note that the CCP loads DDT in over itself, and therefore must be read back in from the disk with a warm boot at the end of the DDT session. As seen in Fig. 8-1A, the CCP gets the file DDT.COM from the disk and loads it into memory. When this is done, the memory allocation becomes what is shown in Fig. 8-1B, where the CCP has been overwritten by the DDT nucleus and the DDT assembly/disassembly portion, which is the second major component of DDT is loaded directly below the nucleus.

Note that DDT is not loaded into memory starting at location 0100H as all other .COM files are! This is so that both DDT and a program starting at 0100H can simultaneously reside in memory. DDT can then be used to debug the program in the TPA. Of course, it is not necessary that the program to be debugged reside at 0100H; it can be anywhere in memory, so long as it does not overwrite either DDT or the BIOS or BDOS modules of CP/M.

Although DDT resides right below BIOS, it is initially loaded into memory at 0100H by the CCP, as all .COM files are, and then it relocates itself upward. This means that whatever is in the lower portion of the TPA will be overwritten by DDT. Thus the program which is to be run concurrently with DDT must be loaded in *after* DDT is loaded so that it will be intact when you want to run it.

When DDT is loaded into memory, it initializes itself, and changes two addresses in the reserved low system memory (below 100H). The first modified address is the jump address contained in memory locations 6 and 7. This is the address of the lowest byte in the BIOS section of CP/M. Many programs read these locations to make sure there is enough room in the TPA for them to operate without overwriting BIOS. To make sure they don't overwrite DDT, this address is changed to be the address of the lowest byte in the DDT nucleus.

However, as you can see, the assemble/disassemble portion can still be written over by a program! If your program checks bytes 6 and 7, and you want to save the assemble/disassemble section of DDT, you might want to change bytes 6 and 7 yourself with DDT to an address below the assemble/disassemble section with some DDT commands which we will show you later.

The second set of addresses that DDT changes are 038H to 03AH. These correspond to the RST 7 (restart) instruction which is recognized by the 8080, 8085, and Z80 microprocessors as a vector to branch to in case of an interrupt. This address is changed to a jump to a breakpoint location in DDT. Thus, if you want to put a software breakpoint in your program, simply place an RST 7 instruction at the desired point, and control will be transferred to DDT when the RST 7 is encountered and executed. Also, a hardware RST 7 can be generated, which will produce the same effect. More on this later as we discuss the breakpoint command.

Once DDT has been invoked by typing the CCP command line

```
A>DDT
```

DDT will respond with the prompt

```
_
```

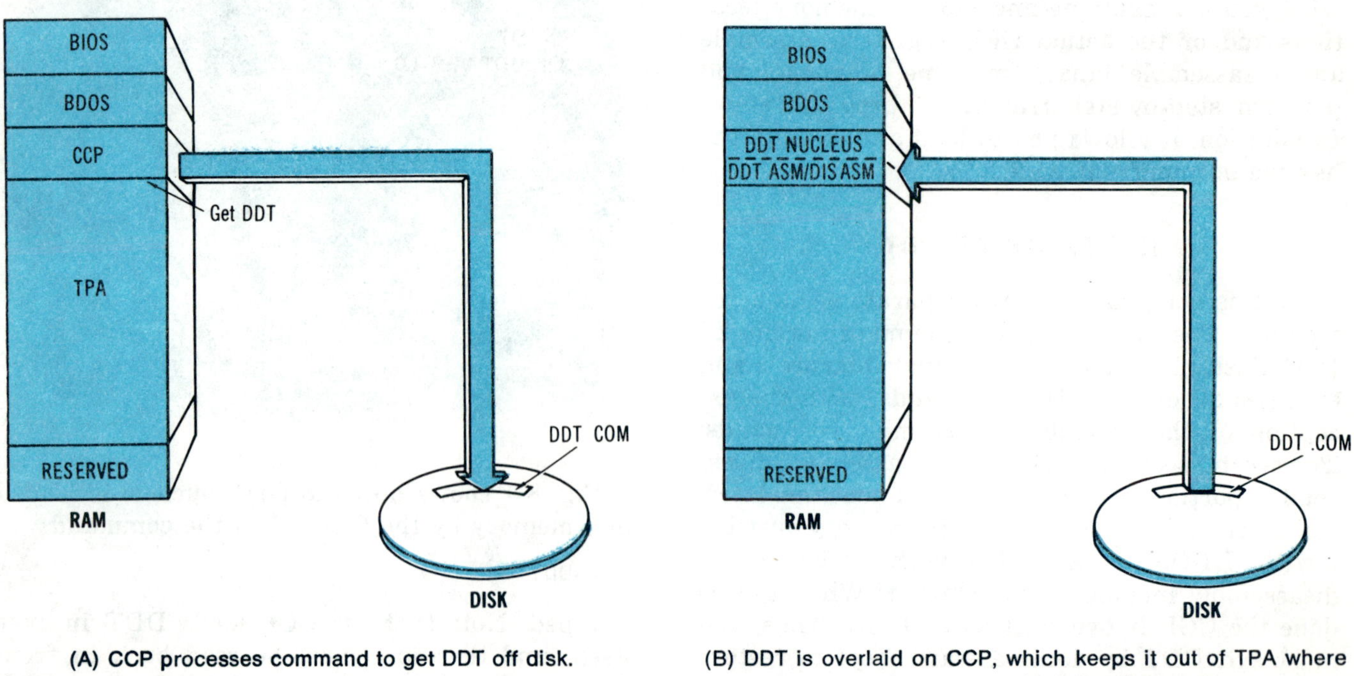

(A) CCP processes command to get DDT off disk.

(B) DDT is overlaid on CCP, which keeps it out of TPA where our program to debug lies.

Fig. 8-1. How DDT overlays the CCP and why a warm boot is required when ending a DDT session.

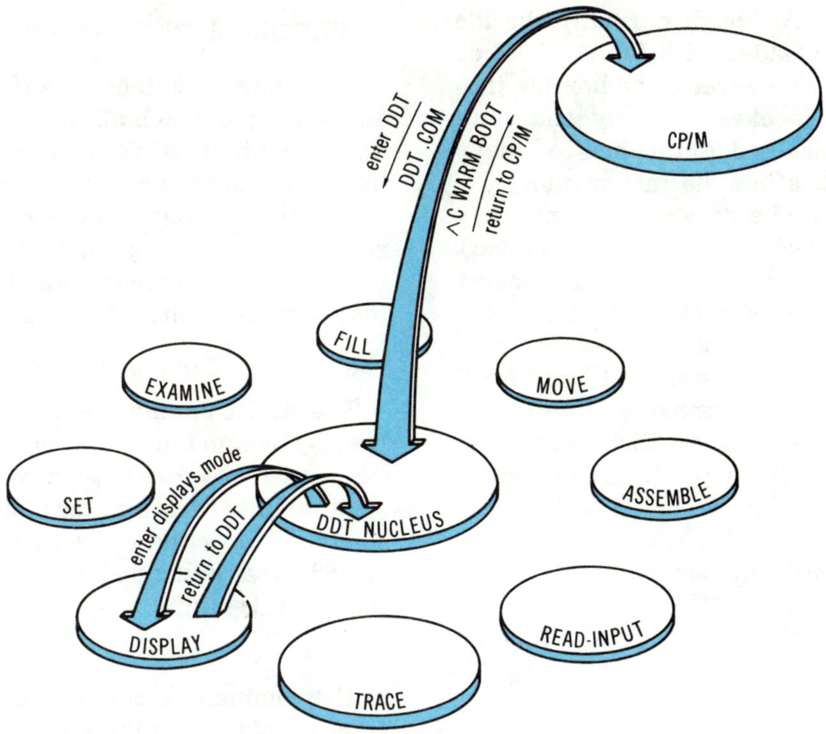

Fig. 8-2. Interaction among DDT, its commands, and CP/M.

as we discussed earlier. This means that we are in the command mode. DDT will at this point recognize a set of fixed commands. These commands allow you to load a file, display memory or CPU register values, assemble or disassemble program instructions, or perform a step-by-step trace of a program's execution.

DDT COMMANDS

From the DDT command mode, you may select one of many DDT submodes to operate in. Once you have entered a command, such as display memory, and you are done with that submode, you must first exit to the command mode again before you go into one of the other submodes. In other words, you cannot transfer directly between submodes; you must go through the command mode each time. A warm boot returns control to CP/M and reloads CCP. Consider each submode as a satellite of the DDT command mode, as shown in Fig. 8-2.

LOADING A FILE

Once DDT itself is loaded into memory, the program to be debugged must be loaded. There are basically two ways to do this. The first allows you to load a file (the program to be debugged) when you load DDT into memory. Instead of simply typing

```
A>DDT
```

as we did in the first example, we can add a file name to the command line, and DDT will load that file into memory before it comes up in the command mode. The following will, for example, load DDT and the hex file TIMER.HEX, which we created in the last chapter, into memory. We will use TIMER.ASM as our test program throughout this chapter. This is done as is shown below. When DDT enters the command mode, DDT will be loaded into memory as well as the Intel hex out-

put file TIMER.HEX. Although normally the file TIMER.HEX must be loaded with LOAD.COM or some other utility which converts the hex file into binary code (which is executable by the computer), DDT automatically does this hex-to-binary conversion as it reads a hex file into memory.

The second way to load a program into memory with DDT is by using the I (Input) and R (Read) commands. The Input command loads a filename into the File Control Block (see Appendix A for an in-depth discussion of File Control Blocks). For the purposes of this discussion, a File Control Block (FCB) is a string of parameters in memory that supervises and controls all disk reads and writes under CP/M. Thus, by placing the filename TIMER.HEX into the FCB, we instruct CP/M to refer all disk read and write commands to the file TIMER.HEX, until further notice (i.e., we change the filename in the FCB). Note, however, that the file must be on the current drive. Thus the command

```
—ITIMER.HEX
```

will load the *filename* TIMER.HEX into the File Control Block (FCB). This filename will remain in the FCB until it is replaced with another filename.

The Read command will then read the .COM or .HEX *file* specified in the FCB into memory. Remember, as long as you don't write over the FCB (which is located in memory from the addresses 005CH-007FH) any number of Read commands may be issued without issuing Input commands in between to set up the FCB, as we mentioned before. The Read command can therefore be used to re-read in a program which you think may have had some instructions inadvertently altered, for instance. The following command will read in TIMER.HEX (since this was the last filename we inputted to the FCB with the I command).

```
—R
```

DDT actually loads in a file when DDT is invoked with a filename in the command line, as we did in the first example, by issuing internally an Input and subsequent Read command. Thus, if you have loaded a program into memory when you load in DDT, the filename is in the FCB and you may re-Read the file in at any time by simply typing

```
—R
```

in the command mode. In other words, the I command isn't needed.

PROGRAM DISPLAY AND MODIFICATION

DDT has an extensive and sophisticated array of commands which allow you to display and modify the contents of your computer's memory. With these commands you can examine the contents of either the computer memory or the actual CPU registers, and change or fill them with new values if you want. Thus, you can change data, program instructions or the actual CPU registers.

The Display Command

The first command you will want to use is the Display command. This command allows you to examine the contents of any memory location or locations in the computer's memory. The Display command lists the contents of memory in blocks of 256 bytes at a time. The memory display is initiated by typing

```
—Ds,f
```

in the command mode where s and f are optional start and finish addresses of the block of memory to be displayed. If no start or finish addresses are specified, DDT starts with 0100H and continues to display lines, 16 at a time, each time the Display command is entered. The contents of memory are always displayed in lines of 16 bytes in the following format

```
aaaa bb bb bb bb bb bb bb bb bb bb bb bb bb bb bb bb
cccccccccccccccc
```

where *aaaa* is the address in hexadecimal of the first byte in the string, *bb* are the 16 bytes of data in hex format, and *cccccccccccccccc* is the ASCII value of each of the 16 bytes. If the value is not an ASCII printing character, DDT represents it with a ".". For example, the value 06H is the ASCII character CRTL-G and DDT will represent it with a "." in the last field since control characters are nonprinting. The value 6FH, however, is the ASCII "o" and DDT will represent it as "o" in the last field.

Thus the left most four characters are an address, (0000 to FFFF), and the bulk of the remaining line is 16 bytes of data in hex format, followed by any ASCII characters. The ASCII character part of the line is a feature of DDT and is not usually found in most memory dump or monitor examine functions. Most computers just dump hex. The ASCII display helps you identify "strings" in memory. If you examine a section of code that has a message imbedded in it, the message will appear in the ASCII columns.

If you type an address in hexadecimal directly after the D in the command, then DDT will start the display at this point instead of the usual 0100H. It will display 16 lines in the format listed above. If a start and stop address is typed in the command, DDT will display the value of all memory locations from the starting address up to the final address. In this mode however, DDT does not display in blocks of 16 lines. Instead, it continuously types lines on the screen until the final address is displayed. Thus, on a long memory display, the values will scroll off the screen. You can type a CRTL-S to stop the display and then restart it by typing another CRTL-S.

If we wanted to display the program TIMER which we assembled in the last chapter, we could load it into memory with the I and R commands and then display it. Since it is assembled to reside at D800H, then the Display command should have this address as the optional start address. This is how this all should look on your computer.

```
A>DDT
32K DDT VER 2.0
-ITIMER.HEX
-R
-DD800
D800 03 5F 23 A0 45 23 03 D8 C9 56 23 ..gy.9.2w..

                    etc.
```

The Set command is similar to the Display command, except that it displays only one memory location at a time, and it allows you to change the value of that memory location if you wish. The form of the command is

```
Sa
```

where a is the address of the memory location you would like displayed. DDT will return the address and current value of the memory location. If you type a carriage return next, the data is not altered. However, if you would like to alter the contents you type in the new value, in hexadecimal format, and DDT will store it in that location. Following a carriage return, either with or without a new value to be stored, DDT will then display the next address in memory, and its location. It will continue in this fashion until either a "." is typed by the user, or an invalid response is encountered. DDT will then revert back to the command mode.

In the following example we will display a memory location, modify it, and then redisplay it so that we can be sure it really was changed.

```
A>DDT TIMER.HEX
32K DDT VER 2.0
-SD800
D800 03 05
D801 5F .
-SD800
D800 05 .
-
```

A command which is very similar to the Set command is the eXamine command. The eXamine command allows you to examine and alter any of the 8080 CPU registers, condition flags, program counter, or stack pointer. The form of the eXamine command is

```
X
```

or

```
Xr
```

where r is a label representing one of the 8080 registers. If no register is specified, DDT will display all of the registers, flags, and counters in the following format.

```
CfZfMfEfIf A=bb B=dddd C=dddd H=dddd S=dddd
                                   P=dddd inst
```

where the capital letters refer to registers, flags, or counters, f is 0 or 1 representing a single bit value of a flag, bb is a single byte value and dddd is a double byte value, and inst is the mnemonic for the current instruction in the memory location contained in the program counter. Table 8-1 lists the symbol for each of the 8080 flags, registers, and counters.

So if we wanted to find out the current state of the accumulator, we would enter the command mode and type

```
-X
```

and DDT would respond with

```
C0Z0M0E0I0 A=FF B=0000 D=0000 H=0000
                      S=0100 P=0100 RST 7
```

Table 8-1. Symbols For 8080 Flags, Registers, and Counters

Flags:	
	115
C Carry Flag	Z Zero Flag
M Minus Flag	E Even parity Flag
I Interdigit Carry Flag	
Registers:	
A Accumulator	B BC register pair
D DE register pair	H HL register pair
Counters and Pointers:	
P Program Counter	S Stack Pointer

In this case all of the flags and CPU registers except the accumulator are zero, the current top of the stack is 0100H, the next instruction to be executed is at memory location 0100H and is an RST 7 instruction, and the accumulator has FFH in it.

The second form of the eXamine command, which we mentioned above, allows you to display and change the current state of any of the flags, registers, or counters in much the same manner as the Set command allowed us to display and change the contents of memory. For example, if we want to change the contents of the Accumulator from FFH to 00H we would issue the following commands

```
A>DDT
32K DDT VER 2.0
-XA
FF 00
-XA
00
-
```

As with the Set command, DDT will wait for your input after it displays the contents of the flag, register, or counter. If you answer with a carriage return, the contents will not be altered. However, if you type in a new value, DDT will update the contents of the flag, register, or counter with the new value. Unlike the Set command, eXamine will not automatically go on to the next register (remember Set automatically displays the next memory location unless you type a "."), but rather returns to the command mode.

Often it is necessary to initialize large blocks of memory to a predetermined value, such as initializing a buffer to some "empty" value. We could of course accomplish this task with some large number of Set commands, but that would be very time consuming. Instead, we could use the Fill command. The Fill command will place data in all memory locations from the starting memory location to the final memory location specified in the command. The form of the Fill command is

```
Fs,f,d
```

where s is the starting address, f is the final address, and d is the new data, in Hex, to be placed in these locations. Thus if we wanted to initialize a buffer to the Hex value E5H and the buffer was 128 bytes long, starting at memory location 0080H, the command would be

```
—F0080,00FF,E5
```

Note that the final address is filled with the value, or in other words, the Fill command fills up to and including the final address.

The Move command is the last of the program display and modification commands. Move allows you to move a block of memory from one location to another. For instance, let's say you decided that for some reason you wanted to move the buffer which we just initialized with the Fill command to another location, say C000H to C4FFH. We could do this with the Move command. The form of the Move command is

```
—Ms,f,d
```

where s is the starting address of the block to be moved, f is the final address of the block to be moved, and d is the starting address of the destination. Thus to move our 128 byte buffer from 0080H to C000H we would issue the following command to DDT

```
—M0080,00FF,C000
```

Again, remember that the move goes up to and includes the final address of the block to be moved, and that you can only move a block of memory up, not down.

Program Assembly and Listing

Often during a debugging session, you will realize that you made a mistake while you were writing your program, and you would like to correct that mistake now, without eXiting DDT, reediting the program source code with ED, reassembling the program with ASM, and then entering DDT again. DDT will allow you to make many of these changes with the Assemble command.

The Assemble command takes the form

```
Am
```

where m is the memory address where the command is to be assembled. DDT will then respond with the address and wait for you to type in an instruction using the standard 8080 mnemonics (see Chapter 6 for a complete listing of the 8080 mnemonics) and absolute hex addresses and constants. DDT will then assemble the code, place the binary machine instruction in memory, print the address of the next instruction, and wait for another command or a carriage return to terminate the assembly session.

The following sample session will examine memory locations 0100H to 01FFH, assemble a CALL instruction at location 0100H, and then reexamine memory to see the change in the memory contents. Notice that DDT recognizes the instruction CALL D800 as a three-byte instruction and therefore displays 0103 as the next address. Had the instruction been, for example, an RST 7 instruction (a single-byte instruction—FFH), the next address displayed would have been 0101.

```
A>DDT
32K DDT VER 2.0
-D0100,01FF
(DISPLAY OF MEMORY)
-A0100
0100 CALL D800
0103
-D0100,01FF
(DISPLAY OF MEMORY)
```

You must remember when working with the Assemble command, that you are assembling in "real time" and that DDT is assembling one line at a time. Thus while your original program may have used equates, pseudo operands and instructions, the DDT assembler cannot use these. Thus the instruction

```
—A0100
0100 CALL SETBUFFER
```

will produce the following response from DDT

```
—A0100
0100 CALL SETBUFFER
?
0100
```

DDT prompts with a "?" whenever an invalid instruction is entered. In the above example, DDT correctly recognized the fact that SETBUFFER is not a valid hex address. However, if you know that the original program contained the equate

```
SETBUFFER        EQU        0D800H
```

and you substitute 0D800H for SETBUFFER so that the command looks like this

```
—A0100
0100 CALL D800
0103
—
```

DDT will recognize and properly assemble the instruction.

The List command is the second command in the Assembler/Disassembler module of DDT. With this command you can list the program you are currently debugging in mnemonic form. The form for the List command is

```
Ls,f
```

where s is an optional starting line number and f is an optional final line number. If no line numbers are given, List will start at the first line of code (determined by the current program counter) and list the next 12 lines. Each successive List command will disassemble 12 more lines of the program. For example, the session at the top of pg. 70 displays the first 12 lines of our program TIMER. Remember, however, from our discussion of the various components of DDT earlier in the chapter that the DDT Assemble/Disassemble module can be overwritten if your program is large. If this is the case, then DDT will simply return a "?" when it is asked to list program lines. Unfortunately, the only solution to this problem is to get more memory into your computer system (assuming that you are not already using 64K), or to make your program small by reprogramming some or all of it.

TRACING PROGRAM EXECUTION

Often when you are debugging a program of one kind or another, it is desirable and necessary to trace the execution of your program step by step to make sure that it is executing the way you had anticipated, or to find out why it is not work-

```
A>DDT
32K DDT VER 2.0
-ITIMER.HEX
-R
NEXT  PC
D824 0000
-LD800
D800  JMP  D804
D803  NOP
D804  PUSH H
D805  PUSH D
D806  PUSH B
D807  PUSH PSW
D808  ORA  A
D809  OUT  F0
D80B  STA  D803
D80E  MVI  B,64
D810  MVI  A,80
-
```

ing. DDT provides the capability to do this with the Trace function. The Trace command takes the form

```
Tn
```

where n is an option number (taken in hexadecimal) representing the number of program steps to be traced. If no number is entered for n, DDT assumes a value of 1 for n, and single steps one instruction.

While using the Trace function, a number of things must be remembered which have a direct bearing on the execution of the program under test. First, Trace implements the "breakpoint" function by executing RST 7 commands. Thus, the user program cannot use this instruction, nor should you place a jump to an interrupt service routine at the RST 7 address (0038H). Secondly, a program under Trace will execute about 500 times slower than real time due to the overhead of the Trace command. Thus programs which execute real time functions, such as our TIMER program, will not operate the same in the Trace mode as they would in normal execution. For example, if we were running the TIMER program with an oscilloscope hooked up to pin 7 of port F0H, we should see a 1 millisecond pulse every time we ran the program. However, if we run TIMER under the DDT Trace function, the pulse on pin 7 will be significantly wider than 1 ms. Still, we would be able to follow exactly the operation of the TIMER program using Trace, to make sure that it is operating correctly.

Trace will display the contents of the CPU registers, counters, and pointers after the execution of each program step. The format of the Trace output is as follows

```
CfZfMfEfIf A=bb B=dddd D=dddd H=dddd S=dddd
                                          P=dddd Inst
```

which is, as you can see, the same format as the eXamine command we discussed earlier. At the end of a trace, DDT will display the next address to be executed with an asterisk.

The following example is a trace of the first 16 steps of the TIMER program (remember, the DDT trace function notes the number of lines in hexadecimal not decimal).

```
A>DDT
32K DDT VER 2.0
-ITIMER.HEX
-R
NEXT PC
D824 0000
-XP
P=0000 D800
-T10
C0Z0M0E0I0  A=00  B=0000  D=0000  H=0000  S=0100
            P=D800  JMP  D804
C0Z0M0E0I0  A=00  B=0000  D=0000  H=0000  S=0100
            P=D804  PUSH  H
C0Z0M0E0I0  A=00  B=0000  D=0000  H=0000  S=00FE
            P=D805  PUSH  D
C0Z0M0E0I0  A=00  B=0000  D=0000  H=0000  S=00FC
            P=D806  PUSH  B
C0Z0M0E0I0  A=00  B=0000  D=0000  H=0000  S=00FA
            P=D807  PUSH  PSW
C0Z0M0E0I0  A=00  B=0000  D=0000  H=0000  S=00F8
            P=D808  XRA  A
C0Z1M0E1I0  A=00  B=0000  D=0000  H=0000  S=00F8
            P=D809  OUT  F0
C0Z1M0E1I0  A=00  B=0000  D=0000  H=0000  S=00F8
            P=D80B  STA  D803
C0Z1M0E1I0  A=00  B=0000  D=0000  H=0000  S=00F8
            P=D80E  MVI  B,64
C0Z1M0E1I0  A=10  B=6400  D=0000  H=0000  S=00F8
            P=D810  MVI  A,80
C0Z1M0E1I0  A=80  B=6400  D=0000  H=0000  S=00F8
            P=D812  OUT  F0
C0Z1M0E1I0  A=80  B=6400  D=0000  H=0000  S=00F8
            P=D814  DCR  B
C0Z0M0E1I1  A=80  B=6300  D=0000  H=0000  S=00F8
            P=D815  NOP
C0Z0M0E1I1  A=80  B=6300  D=0000  H=0000  S=00F8
            P=D816  NOP
C0Z0M0E1I1  A=80  B=6300  D=0000  H=0000  S=00F8
            P=D817  NOP
C0Z0M0E1I1  A=80  B=6300  D=0000  H=0000  S=00F8
            P=D818  NOP  ★D819
-
```

The Untrace Command

The final DDT command is the Untrace command. It is identical in function to the Trace command, with the exception that it does not display the state of the CPU after every instruction. So you might ask, what does it do, recalling that the output of Trace was mostly data about the CPU state. Untrace allows you to run a program under control of DDT, so that it does not run away on you. For example, if you wanted to trace the last portion of a long program, you could use the Untrace function to get you to the end under control of DDT, and then use the Trace function to watch the execution of the program. In many cases of course, you could simply set the program counter to the address of the section of the program you wanted to debug and then use the Trace function. However, many programs require certain variables to be initialized, and skipping over the initialization section of the program will often lead to invalid results if the rest of the program is run uninitialized. Thus, the Untrace function is the only way to quickly run through a long section of code under the control of DDT.

The form of the Untrace command is identical to the Trace function and is Un, where n is the number of steps to Untrace. Untrace will always display the first line of code that it executes in the same manner as Trace. However, it will stop displaying the program steps at this point and will continue to execute program steps for the number of steps given by n (n is in hexadecimal again). When it has run through the required number of steps, it will display the next value of the program counter, and exit to the command mode. The following example is the same as we did for the Trace function, but we will use the Untrace mode this time.

```
A>DDT
32K DDT VER 2.0
-ITIMER.HEX
-R
NEXT PC
D824 0000
-XP
P=0000 D800
-U10
C0Z0M0E0I0  A=00 B=0000 D=0000 H=0000 S=0100
            P=D800 JMP D804
  *D819
-
```

A SAMPLE DDT SESSION

In this final part of this chapter, we will follow a sample DDT session with the TIMER program we wrote in the last chapter. The actual screen output that you should see from this session is shown in Fig. 8-3. The numbers in the left margin are reference marks for items which we will be discussing as we go through this sample session.

The session starts by loading DDT into memory, and then loading the hex file for the program TIMER in with the Input and Read commands (1). Next we need to set the program counter to the starting address of TIMER. We do this with the eXamine command. Finally, we need to set the number of milliseconds we want TIMER to count, since we are not calling TIMER from a BASIC program which has initialized COUNT with a POKE statement. We do this with the Set command (2).

Now that we have initialized everything, we are ready to begin our trace. We start by tracing the first 16 (Hexadecimal 10) program steps. This gets us through the program initialization part and into the timing loop (3). However, we notice that we have made a mistake, and used the DCX (decrement register pair) instruction instead of the DCR (decrement register) instruction when we are decrementing our loop count (4). We can see this with DDT because the B double register contains 6401H after this instruction instead of 6302H as it should.

We can now use the DDT Assemble command to fix the problem without exiting DDT, changing the source code, and reassembling TIMER. We change the instruction at 7815H from DCX B to DCR B with the Assemble command and we are back in business and ready to test the program again (5).

However, before we Trace the program again, we must remember that we have run 16 program steps already, and some of the machine registers, counters, and pointers are not what they were when we entered the program. In order to correct this we use the eXamine command to restore the initial values for the stack pointer, program counter, accumulator, and register pair B (6).

Now that we have corrected our mistake and reinitialized the CPU and memory, we will run the program again under the Trace command. After looking at the first trace, we can see that the trace did not get completely through the first execution of the timing loop. Therefore, on this trace we will increase the number of steps to be run to 21 (15 hexadecimal) (7).

After running through this trace, and seeing that the program appears to be working as it is supposed to do, we will take a short cut. We could, of course, continue tracing the program execution through all of its iterations through the timing loop; however, this is an extremely tedious and time-consuming process. We will use the eXamine command to decrement the millisecond and loop

```
    A>DDT
    32K DDT VER 2.0
(1) -ITIMER.HEX
    -R
(2) NEXT PC
    D82B 0000
    -XP
    P=0000 D800
    -SD803
    D803 00 02
    D804 E5 .
(3) -T10
    C0Z0M0E0I0  A=00  B=0000  D=0000  H=0000  S=0100  P=D800  JMP   D804
    C0Z0M0E0I0  A=00  B=0000  D=0000  H=0000  S=0100  P=D804  PUSH  H
    C0Z0M0E0I0  A=00  B=0000  D=0000  H=0000  S=00FE  P=D805  PUSH  D
    C0Z0M0E0I0  A=00  B=0000  D=0000  H=0000  S=00FC  P=D806  PUSH  B
    C0Z0M0E0I0  A=00  B=0000  D=0000  H=0000  S=00FA  P=D807  PUSH  PSW
    C0Z0M0E0I0  A=00  B=0000  D=0000  H=0000  S=00F8  P=D808  XRA   A
    C0Z1M0E1I0  A=00  B=0000  D=0000  H=0000  S=00F8  P=D809  OUT   F0
    C0Z1M0E1I0  A=00  B=0000  D=0000  H=0000  S=00F8  P=D80B  LDA   D803
    C0Z1M0E1I0  A=02  B=0000  D=0000  H=0000  S=00F8  P=D80E  MOV   C,A
    C0Z1M0E1I0  A=02  B=0002  D=0000  H=0000  S=00F8  P=D80F  MVI   B,64
    C0Z1M0E1I0  A=02  B=6402  D=0000  H=0000  S=00F8  P=D811  MVI   A,80
    C0Z1M0E1I0  A=80  B=6402  D=0000  H=0000  S=00F8  P=D813  OUT   F0
(4) C0Z1M0E1I0  A=80  B=6402  D=0000  H=0000  S=00F8  P=D815  DCX   B
    C0Z0M0E1I1  A=80  B=6401  D=0000  H=0000  S=00F8  P=D816  NOP
    C0Z0M0E1I1  A=80  B=6401  D=0000  H=0000  S=00F8  P=D817  NOP
    C0Z0M0E1I1  A=80  B=6401  D=0000  H=0000  S=00F8  P=D818  NOP   ★D819
(5) -AD815
    D815  DCR B
    D816
(6) -XP
    P=D819 D800
    -XS
    S=00F8 0100
    -XA
    A=80 00
    -XB
    B=6401 0000
(7) -T15
    C0Z0M0E0I0  A=00  B=0000  D=0000  H=0000  S=0100  P=D800  JMP   D804
    C0Z0M0E0I0  A=00  B=0000  D=0000  H=0000  S=0100  P=D804  PUSH  H
    C0Z0M0E0I0  A=00  B=0000  D=0000  H=0000  S=00FE  P=D805  PUSH  D
    C0Z0M0E0I0  A=00  B=0000  D=0000  H=0000  S=00FC  P=D806  PUSH  B
    C0Z0M0E0I0  A=00  B=0000  D=0000  H=0000  S=00FA  P=D807  PUSH  PSW
    C0Z0M0E0I0  A=00  B=0000  D=0000  H=0000  S=00F8  P=D808  XRA   A
    C0Z1M0E1I0  A=00  B=0000  D=0000  H=0000  S=00F8  P=D809  OUT   F0
    C0Z1M0E1I0  A=00  B=0000  D=0000  H=0000  S=00F8  P=D80B  LDA   D803
    C0Z1M0E1I0  A=02  B=0000  D=0000  H=0000  S=00F8  P=D80E  MOV   C,A
    C0Z1M0E1I0  A=02  B=0002  D=0000  H=0000  S=00F8  P=D80F  MVI   B,64
    C0Z1M0E1I0  A=02  B=6402  D=0000  H=0000  S=00F8  P=D811  MVI   A,80
    C0Z1M0E1I0  A=80  B=6402  D=0000  H=0000  S=00F8  P=D813  OUT   F0
    C0Z1M0E1I0  A=80  B=6402  D=0000  H=0000  S=00F8  P=D815  DCR   B
    C0Z0M0E1I1  A=80  B=6302  D=0000  H=0000  S=00F8  P=D816  NOP
    C0Z0M0E1I1  A=80  B=6302  D=0000  H=0000  S=00F8  P=D817  NOP
    C0Z0M0E1I1  A=80  B=6302  D=0000  H=0000  S=00F8  P=D818  NOP
    C0Z0M0E1I1  A=80  B=6302  D=0000  H=0000  S=00F8  P=D819  NOP
    C0Z0M0E1I1  A=80  B=6302  D=0000  H=0000  S=00F8  P=D81A  JNZ   D815
    C0Z0M0E1I1  A=80  B=6302  D=0000  H=0000  S=00F8  P=D815  DCR   B
    C0Z0M0E1I1  A=80  B=6202  D=0000  H=0000  S=00F8  P=D816  NOP
    C0Z0M0E1I1  A=80  B=6202  D=0000  H=0000  S=00F8  P=D817  NOP   ★D818
```

Fig. 8-3. Tracing our sample

counts ourselves, instead of letting the program run on to do this. We will set them both to 1 so that we can watch the execution of the program as it exits the loop to make sure that there are no other problems (8).

We now have 19 more steps to go for the program to complete, since we have set the counters to 1 (don't worry, we cheated and counted them out first for this example; we didn't have any idea how many at first either). We enter the Trace mode again and look at the next 19 steps (9). As you can see, we successfully exit the timing loop, restore all CPU registers to their value prior to the BASIC program calling this program, and return to the BASIC program (10).

Finally, we exit the session back to the CP/M CCP by typing a CRTL-C to force a warm boot. At this point, we can be relatively certain that TIMER works as it is supposed to. However, the DDT can only take you so far in the process of debugging a program. Often, program errors occur in the initial flow or logic which the program was written to, and not in the program coding. DDT will do well in catching and correcting the latter errors, but the former kind must be found and corrected by the programmer.

As you can see DDT allows you to get into the "real guts" of the CPU's operation. With DDT, and some practice, you should be able to debug the most difficult assembly language programs.

```
(8)    -XB
       B=6202 0101
(9)    -T13
       C0Z0M0E0I1  A=80  B=0101  D=0000  H=0000  S=00F8  P=D818  NOP
       C0Z0M0E0I1  A=80  B=0101  D=0000  H=0000  S=00F8  P=D819  NOP
       C0Z0M0E0I1  A=80  B=0101  D=0000  H=0000  S=00F8  P=D81A  JNZ   D815
       C0Z0M0E0I1  A=80  B=0101  D=0000  H=0000  S=00F8  P=D815  DCR   B
       C0Z1M0E1I1  A=80  B=0001  D=0000  H=0000  S=00F8  P=D816  NOP
       C0Z1M0E1I1  A=80  B=0001  D=0000  H=0000  S=00F8  P=D817  NOP
       C0Z1M0E1I1  A=80  B=0001  D=0000  H=0000  S=00F8  P=D818  NOP
       C0Z1M0E1I1  A=80  B=0001  D=0000  H=0000  S=00F8  P=D819  NOP
       C0Z1M0E1I1  A=80  B=0001  D=0000  H=0000  S=00F8  P=D81A  JNZ   D815
       C0Z1M0E1I1  A=80  B=0001  D=0000  H=0000  S=00F8  P=D81D  MVI   B,64
       C0Z1M0E1I1  A=80  B=6401  D=0000  H=0000  S=00F8  P=D81F  DCR   C
       C0Z1M0E1I1  A=80  B=6400  D=0000  H=0000  S=00F8  P=D820  JNZ   D815
       C0Z1M0E1I1  A=80  B=6400  D=0000  H=0000  S=00F8  P=D823  XRA   A
       C0Z1M0E1I0  A=00  B=6400  D=0000  H=0000  S=00F8  P=D824  OUT   F0
       C0Z1M0E1I0  A=00  B=6400  D=0000  H=0000  S=00F8  P=D826  POP   PSW
       C0Z1M0E1I0  A=00  B=6400  D=0000  H=0000  S=00FA  P=D827  POP   B
       C0Z1M0E1I0  A=00  B=0000  D=0000  H=0000  S=00FC  P=D828  POP   D
       C0Z1M0E1I0  A=00  B=0000  D=0000  H=0000  S=00FE  P=D829  POP   H
       C0Z1M0E1I0  A=00  B=0000  D=0000  H=0000  S=0100  P=D82A  RET
(10)   -^C
       A>
```

timing loop program with DDT.

SAVING YOUR PROGRAM

Once you have finished debugging your program with DDT, it needs to be stored on the disk. As you recall from our discussion of ASM, the compiled program stored in the .HEX file cannot be run by your computer. DDT has a mechanism for converting a program from .HEX format into binary object code.

Since we don't want to have to use DDT every time we want to run a program, then we must somehow accomplish this conversion without DDT. This is the purpose of the LOAD utility. LOAD will convert a .HEX file into object code and store it as a .COM file.

Thus if we were to invoke LOAD to convert our sample program into a .COM file we would type

```
A>LOAD TIMER
```

and LOAD would read in TIMER.HEX and convert it into binary object code and write it back onto the disk as TIMER.COM. Note that LOAD does not erase TIMER.HEX; it will still be on the disk.

The second way of saving a program is with the CCP SAVE command. This is a much more limited way, since you have to know how many pages (256 byte block) long the program is, and the program must begin at 0100H. However, in many cases it can be the best way to get a binary object code file. For example, if your program started at 0100H, and you had done some extensive modifications of the program with DDT (using the Assemble directive, etc.) you could store the resulting program, without having to go back and edit the original source code, recompile it with ASM, and then convert it from hex format to binary object code with LOAD.

We encourage you to play around with both methods and become familiar with them. There are no real clear-cut rules for when to use which method.

Appendix **A**

The Internal Structure of CP/M

The CP/M operating system is an extremely powerful and flexible operating system. With it, many different types of programs can be run on many different types of machines. CP/M accomplishes this task by setting up a standard protocol or method of communication so that all programs, whether they are BASIC interpreters, word processors, or any other application program or utility, will be able to run under CP/M.

All commands to CP/M from a program are accomplished through what is referred to as "system calls." System calls are routines in CP/M which perform specific "low level" functions like getting a character from the keyboard or displaying text on the crt. An 8080 *CALL* instruction, sent from the program, initiates the desired routine. System calls are used in the program whenever control of the computer is passed over to CP/M to accomplish a specific task. Control is returned to the program by CP/M when the task is complete. For example, let's say a program wants to output a character to the current console device. At the appropriate output point in the program, the character to be output to the console device, and the proper command number (CP/M recognizes many system calls, thus the program uses a number to distinguish which one it wants performed) are passed to CP/M along with control of the computer. When CP/M returns from the system call to the program, the character will have been output to the console device (such as a crt screen).

As you can see from the example listed above, this arrangement saves the program from having to be modified for each particular machine that the program must be run on. Instead of the program having to know what the console device is (i.e., is it a printer, crt, etc.), where it is located in memory or what port or ports it is on, and how to talk to it, the program simply issues a system call to output a character to the console device, and CP/M's BIOS or BDOS takes care of the rest. It is this concept of system calls that makes CP/M as flexible and widely used as it is.

GENERALIZED SYSTEM CALL

There is a general form to all system calls whether they are a simple i/o command such as output a character to the console or list device, or whether they are a more complicated disk command such as read a file record. In order to understand the general form of a system call a few preliminaries must be covered.

First, as we mentioned earlier, system calls are accomplished by executing an 8080 CALL instruction to the CP/M entry point, which is contained in the reserved memory area below 0100H. The entry point is located at 0005H and is a JMP instruction to the **actual** CP/M entry point in BIOS (recall the CP/M BIOS and BDOS modules are the parts of CP/M which execute the system calls). The entry point is implemented this way, however, so that a program operating under CP/M does not have to keep track of how big a system it is running under. Because CP/M resides in the top portion of memory, the actual entry point will be different for each size system. For a 32K system the entry point in BIOS may be 7A28H, whereas for a 48K system, that entry point would be higher up at BA28H. CP/M makes sure that the JMP address at 0005H is always correct. Part of the MOVCPM utility changes this address whenever a new CP/M system image is being created for a different size memory. Thus calls will always have the same entry point, 0005H.

There are many system calls supported by CP/M. You can consult your CP/M manuals for a detailed description of these calls. Table A-1 summarizes these calls. Because of the large number of system calls supported by CP/M, a general protocol has been established, which all of the system calls fit into. The protocol deals basically with the passing of information to and from the CP/M operating system by the calling program. There are several types of information which will go back and forth between your program and CP/M, and each type of information, or parameter, is passed in a specific manner.

When a program issues a CALL instruction, the most common place where information can be passed is in the internal registers of the CPU. If the amount of information that needs to be passed back and forth can't be stored in the registers, then the protocol specifies that a "block" of memory be set up with the information in it and *the address of that block of memory be passed in the registers.* We will examine "parameter blocks" in greater detail later on when we discuss the File Control Block and disk i/o commands.

The first piece of information which must be passed to the CP/M operating system is the specific call which the program would like CP/M to execute. Each of the system calls is assigned a number, and that number is *placed in the C register prior to executing the CALL instruction* to get to CP/M. CP/M will read the C register, determine which call was requested, and then execute that call. (See Table A-1.)

Often, as we mentioned, we need to pass information to the operating system in addition to the number of the system call we would like performed. Consider the system call which prints a character to the console device; we will not only need the system call number, but the character to be printed will also have to be passed. Another example would be the system call which changes the beginning memory address of the disk i/o buffer which CP/M uses for all disk read and write operations. In this case we would need to

Table A-1. CP/M System Call Summary

Function Number	Description
*0	Resets CP/M operating system
1	Console input (unbuffered)
2	Console output (unbuffered)
3	Reader device input
4	Punch device output
5	List output
*6	Direct console I/O
7	Get I/O status byte
8	Set I/O status byte
9	Print a string to the console
10	Read console buffer
11	Get console status
*12	Return version number
13	Reset disk drive
14	Select disk
15	Open file
16	Close file
17	Search for first occurrence of filename
18	Search for next occurrence of filename
19	Delete file
20	Read a record sequentially
21	Write a record sequentially
22	Create a file
23	Rename a file
24	Return the disk log-in vector address
25	Return current disk drive number
26	Set disk I/O buffer address
27	Get allocation map address
*28	Write a protected disk
*29	Get Read Only vector address
*30	Set file attributes
*31	Get disk parameter table address
*32	Set/Get user code
*33	Read a record in random access
*34	Write a record in random access
*35	Compute file size
*36	Set random record field in FCB

*Implemented in version 2.0 or later only

pass a 16-bit address to CP/M, as well as pass the system call number.

In general, 8-bit values, such as characters to be output to the console device, are passed *from* CP/M to the calling program in the Accumulator (Reg A), and *to* CP/M in register E. The 16-bit values, such as addresses, are passed in registers pair D (Regs D and E).

The program shown in Fig. A-1 shows how a typical system call is done. The CONOUT system call is number 2 and the SETDMA call is number 26. This program will set the disk i/o buffer to 2000H and then output an asterisk ("*") character to the Console when it is done.

Here's how the program performs the i/o using the system calls. The statement at the very beginning of the program (ORG 0100H) tells the CP/M assembler ASM what the beginning address of this program shall be, i.e., where to start generating object code. Following this are six equate (EQU) directives which assign values to the six variables at the left. The variable or symbolic name CONOUT becomes the value 2, SETDMA is 26, and so on. The entry point for all calls is 0005H and we call this ENTRY. BUFFER becomes 2000H as we desire. Next, the label START indicates the beginning of the actual code that does the work. LXI D,BUFFER puts the value of BUFFER (2000H, a 16-bit value) in the DE register while the next instruction, MVI C,SETDMA, puts the value of

```
        ORG     0100H       ;MAKE A .COM FILE
CONOUT  EQU     2           ;PRINT A CHACTER TO
                            ;THE CONSOLE
SETDMA  EQU     26          ;RESET DMA BUFFER
                            ;ADDRESS
ASTER   EQU     2AH         ;ASCII "*" CHARACTER
BOOT    EQU     0000H       ;WARM BOOT ENTRY
ENTRY   EQU     0005H       ;CP/M ENTRY POINT
BUFFER  EQU     2000H       ;NEW BUFFER ADDRESS
        ;
START:  LXI     D,BUFFER    ;LOAD NEW BUFFER
                            ;ADDRESS TO D AND E
        MVI     C,SETDMA    ;LOAD SYSTEM CALL
        CALL    ENTRY       ;CALL CP/M
        ;
        MVI     E,ASTER     ;LOAD THE "*" CHAR
                            ;INTO REG E
        MVI     C,CONOUT    ;LOAD SYSTEM CALL
        CALL    ENTRY       ;CALL CP/M
        ;
        JMP     BOOT        ;EXIT AND WARM BOOT
        ;
        END
```

Fig. A-1. An example of how a simple system call works.

SETDMA (26) in the C-register. (We use MVI because this is a single 8-bit value.) Finally the instruction CALL ENTRY is executed and the program transfers control to the instruction at address 0005H, which in turn jumps to the CP/M entry point. The BDOS module gets the function number from the C-register, the buffer address from the DE pair and does its thing. Control is returned to our program in Fig. A-1, and the next instruction, MVI E,ASTER is executed. It loads an ASCII asterisk character ("*") (its hex value=2A) into the E-register. Next we do an MVI C,CONOUT to load the C register with the function number for a CONOUT system call (see Table A-1) which is 2. Finally we do a CALL ENTRY to perform the actual system call to output the * character to the cosnole device. system call to output the * character to the console device. Finally the program ends with a JMP BOOT instruction which jumps to locations 0000H and causes CP/M to perform a warm boot (similar to typing a control-C).

BASIC I/O SYSTEM CALLS

CP/M supports two different kinds of system calls. The first are what we call basic i/o system calls, which deal with input and output of the four logical i/o devices supported by CP/M (see Chapter 2 for more on the CP/M logical i/o devices). The second kind are the disk i/o system calls which provide the interface between your programs and the CP/M disk file structure.

The basic i/o system calls provide for the input and output of characters using one of the four logical i/o devices. (As you remember, only the CONSOLE device supports both input and output. The LIST and PUNCH devices are output only, while the READER is an input only device.) In order to call these functions from your program, the appropriate system call number must be put in the C register, and the ASCII character to be output (if it is an output system call) in register E, prior to issuing the system call. Of course, in the case of the input calls no character need be put in register E. When CP/M returns control of the computer to your program, the Accumulator (register A) will contain the ASCII character which was input.

Buffered I/O

In addition to the input/output functions described above, CP/M supports the input and output of character strings (one or more characters) through the CONSOLE device. This allows your programs to input or output a string of characters with one system call, instead of issuing a system call for each character.

These string-type system calls are referred to as *buffered* i/o. In order to print a string of characters to the CONSOLE device, the string must first be set up in memory and terminated with the "$" character. The starting memory address of the string is placed in registers D and E and the system call number (9) is placed in register C. CP/M will then start at the first memory location (contained in DE) and output each successive character to the CONSOLE until the "$" is encountered.

The string input system call is very similar in nature. Your program should set a location in memory where it wants the string to be placed by CP/M after being input (this buffer should be at least 256 bytes in length). The starting address of this buffer is passed to CP/M in registers D and E. CP/M will then place all characters input to the CONSOLE device in successive memory locations until a carriage return/line feed is encountered or until the buffer overflows (more that 256 characters are input). One of the main reasons that the string input command is used is that the usual CP/M line editing commands (see Chapter 3) are supported by the string input system call, thus eliminating this editing burden from your program.

Changing the I/O Status Byte

CP/M keeps track of the current logical i/o device assignments (see Chapter 3) in what is called the i/o status byte which is stored in memory address 0004H. In most cases, we use the STAT utility to change the current assignments. However, there are times when it is necessary for a program to change the various assignments dynamically. CP/M allows a program to do this with the Get and Set i/o status byte system calls. In the case of the Get i/o byte call, the current value of the i/o byte is returned in register A by the system call. The Set i/o byte call writes the value in register E to the i/o status byte memory location (0004H).

Direct CONSOLE Access

CP/M provides two system calls to allow you to access the CONSOLE device directly, i.e., without buffering or the usual CP/M line editing commands. The first system call, Get CONSOLE Status, allows you to determine if a character has been typed at the CONSOLE. If a character has been typed, then the value 0FFH is returned in register A; otherwise, 00H is returned.

The second call is a direct console i/o call, but is only supported under CP/M version 2.0 and later. This will allow your program to perform i/o directly to and from the CONSOLE device in those special applications where regular CONSOLE i/o would cause problems with your program. The Direct CONSOLE i/o system call is different than the other logical device system calls in that the same call supports both input and output. If register E contains the value 0FFH, then CP/M assumes an input is being requested, and returns the next character input to the CONSOLE in register A. If register E contains anything but 0FFH, then CP/M assumes an output call is being requested, and will output the value in E to the CONSOLE device.

Other Basic System Calls

There are two more basic system calls supported only by CP/M versions 2.0 and later. The Return version number system call will return the current CP/M version number in register L. CP/M returns the version number in hexadecimal form, starting with 20H for version 2.0. Version 2.1 would be returned as 21H and so on up to 2FH. All releases of CP/M prior to 2.0 will return 00H in the L register.

The final basic system call is the System reset call. This call is issued when a program has finished execution and wants to execute a warm boot and return system control to the CCP. This call is identical in operation to issuing a JMP 0000H instruction, which is the way programs running under versions 1.4 and earlier execute a warm boot (this is still a valid way to execute a warm boot under version 2.0 and later).

DISK I/O SYSTEM CALLS

The disk i/o system calls are similar in structure to the basic i/o calls. The call number is placed in the C register and the CP/M entry point (0005H) is called. However, with the basic i/o calls, we were usually only dealing with one character at one time. Therefore we could usually pass all of the necessary data to and from CP/M and the calling program in the internal CPU registers (with the exception of the buffered input and output calls). With the disk i/o we are dealing with much larger blocks of data, usually 128 bytes, and therefore we cannot use the internal CPU registers to pass data. In addition, the complexity of the CP/M file structure requires too many parameters to pass them in the registers.

CP/M sets up two memory blocks to pass data and parameters back and forth between the calling program and the disk. The first block, the disk data buffer, a 128-byte block of memory (which can be located anywhere in memory), is used for all disk read and write operations. The second block is the File Control Block (FCB), which is a 33-byte (36 bytes under version 2.0 and later) block of memory used to pass parameters which control the disk i/o to and from CP/M. The FCB can also be located anywhere in memory. The FCB is used very much like the CP/M registers are used for passing parameters.

The FCB format is shown in Fig. A-2. Each field in the FCB must be filled in properly before a disk system call is issued. In general, the first 13 bytes are the responsibility of the programmer to maintain; i.e., these are the bytes used to pass the required information on to CP/M as to what file should be accessed. Bytes 13 through 31 are maintained by CP/M, and may be read by your program, but you should not change them. The FCB is usually located in memory starting at 005CH. However, it can be located anywhere the programmer wishes, provided, of course, that it does not interfere with some other system module.

The CP/M File Structure

Records—CP/M files are constructed from basic building blocks called *records*. A record is a 128-byte block of data containing either program object code, program data, or text. A file is therefore simply a number of these records which are grouped together and given a name. Since a file can have a very large number of these records in it (under version 2.0 there can be as many as 65,536 records in each file), CP/M must impose a higher level of internal structure to manage all of the records in a file.

Extents—CP/M does this managing with a logical data block called an *extent*. An extent is 128 records, which is the equivalent of 16,384 bytes of data. Therefore, a CP/M file is comprised of at least one, and often more than one, extent. The reason why CP/M uses extents has to do with the way it keeps track of *where* all of the records of a file are located on a disk.

Allocation Units—A standard 8-inch CP/M floppy disk has 250K bytes ($K = 1024$) of storage space on it (128 bytes per sector X 26 sectors per track $\times$ 77 tracks per side $= 256{,}256$ bytes). Thus, there are 2002 ($26 \times 77 = 2002$) sectors where CP/M could store a 128-byte record of a file. In order to keep track of where 2002 sectors are, the diskette is broken up into *allocation units*, where an allocation unit is 8 sectors or 1024 bytes of information. Since

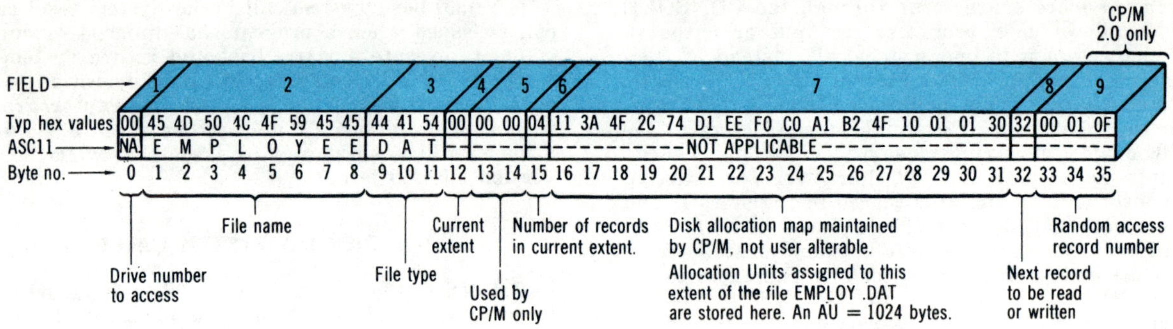

FCB LAYOUT - Usually sits at 005CH in memory.

Field	Byte	Description
1	0	Drive number to access 0 = currently logged disk 1 = drive A: 2 = drive B: etc.
2	1-8	File name padded with blanks.
3	9-11	File type padded with blanks.
4	12	Current extent. Usually set to 0.
5	13-14	Used internally by CP/M. Should be set to 0,0 by the user.
6	15	Number of records in the current extent (byte 12).
7	16-31	Disk allocation map. Maintained by CP/M. Should not be changed by the user.
8	32	Next record to be read or written. Under version 2.0 this applies to sequential access only
9	33-35	Version 2.0 and later only. Random access record number. Bytes 33-34 contain a 16-bit number in the range of 0 to 65535. Byte 35 must be 0 or an error will result.

Fig. A-2. CP/M format for the disk File Control Block or FCB.

the CP/M operating system image is stored in the first two tracks (tracks 0 and 1) of the diskette, the actual data storage area starts with Track 2, Sector 1 (for some reason, tracks are numbered 0–76, while sectors are numbered 1–26). This is the beginning of the first allocation unit which includes the first 8 sectors. The allocation units are consecutively numbered until the last sector on the disk (Track 76, Sector 26) has been included in an allocation unit. There would then be a total of 243 complete allocation units on a standard 8-inch diskette (128 bytes per sector × 26 sectors per track × 75 tracks / 1024 bytes per allocation unit = 243.75 allocation units). Thus we have allocation units 1 to 243 since we can't have a 0.75 allocation unit.

Each time a CP/M file needs more space to write more records to, a new allocation unit is assigned to it giving the file 1024 new bytes even though only 128 may actually be used. For example, if a file has 16 records in it, and we need to write the 17th record, CP/M will assign a new allocation unit to the file, since the previous two allocation units are now filled up. This new allocation unit will store record 17 up to record 24 of the file even though only record 17 is currently written. Each extent can have up to 16 allocation units assigned to it. The *number* of each allocation unit assigned to an extent is stored in one of the bytes in field 7 of the FCB (bytes 16-31), one byte per allocation unit.

CP/M keeps a master list in memory of all of the assigned allocation units currently assigned to a file and all of the unused allocation units. Whenever a new allocation unit is required by a file, CP/M will take the next available allocation unit, delete it from the unused list and add it to the FCB of the file, as well as to the assigned allocation unit list in memory. These lists are read into BDOS from the diskette the first time the diskette is accessed after a warm system boot. By assigning new allocation units to files as they get larger, and reclaiming (into the unused allocation unit list) allocation units as files get smaller, or are erased altogether, CP/M can dynamically manage all of the file space on a diskette. And a file's data can be spread across the disk in randomly located sectors.

Directory—The final mechanism used by CP/M to keep track of the files on a diskette is the directory. CP/M stores the directory information in the beginning of the data storage area of the diskette (Track 2, Sector 1). *The directory contains an entry for each extent of each file.* Thus, a file with more than one extent will have multiple directory entries, although when you issue a CCP DIR command, only the first directory entry for each file is displayed. The directory entry is actually a copy of the first 32 bytes of the FCB for that given extent! A quick glance back at the FCB description will show that the first 32 bytes contain the file name, extent, and allocation unit map of the extent. In a standard CP/M system, there is space allocated for 64 directory entries. Since each directory entry takes up 32 bytes, the directory takes up the first two allocation units of the data storage space (64 entries × 32 bytes per entry = 2048 bytes = 2 allocation units).

Example. In order to summarize what we have described here, we will take a look at a representative disk system call, and show you the steps that CP/M goes through. Lets assume we want to read the 167th record of the file EMPLOYEE.DAT, a file containing employee data for a payroll application program. In order to access this record under CP/M version 1.4 or earlier, we would have to convert the 167th record into an extent/record designation (since there are 128 records in each extent, this would be the 2nd extent, 39th record); with version 2.0 or later, we can ask for the 167th record and CP/M will do the conversion for us. The FCB for the file is shown in Fig. A-2.

Since we want the second extent, CP/M will then go to the disk directory and get the second directory entry for the file EMPLOYEE.DAT. It will then look in the allocation map (bytes 16-31 of the FCB/directory entry) to find the allocation unit which contains the desired record. Since there are 8 sectors or records per allocation unit, the 39th record would be in the 5th allocation unit assigned to that extent (39 / 8 = 5). Thus, CP/M will look at byte 20 in the FCB/directory entry for the allocation unit number (16..17..18..19..20). We will assume that the record is contained in the 117th allocation unit (i.e., byte 20 was 74H), although it could be in any allocation unit. The 39th record of the file will then be the 7th record in the 117th allocation unit. In order to find the actual track/sector address, CP/M needs to find the start of the 117th allocation unit and then add 7 sectors to it. This would be the 37th track, 25th sector (116 allocation units × 8 sectors per allocation unit + 7 sectors = 935th sector of the data storage area). Thus, 35 tracks × 26 sectors per track = 910 sectors which is a little under our 935 sectors, so 935 sectors − 910 sectors = 25th sector of the 35th track of the data storage area. This sector begins with the second track, so this finally comes to the 37th track (35 + 2), 25th sector of the diskette. Whew!!

Having done all of this work, CP/M will then issue a command to the disk drive controller instructing it to read the sector with the address track 37, sector 25. The controller will then read this 128-byte sector, and store the information in the disk i/o buffer in memory. When all of this is complete, then CP/M will return from the system call and return control to the program. The required information is now in the memory buffer awaiting your program's use of it.

File Maintenance System Calls

In order to properly keep track of the files on a disk, CP/M requires that some preliminary system calls be issued by a program *before* actual read/write operation is possible.

Creating, Deleting, and Renaming Files—If a file does not already exist on a disk, it must be created first with the Make File system call. This call makes a directory entry on the disk for the file. Once a file has been created, it can then be accessed by your program. Note that a file need only be created once. CP/M will automatically create new directory entries for each new extent as they are required. This saves you from having to issue a Make File system call every time your file grows to the point where another extent is required. Once a file has been created, it can be erased with the Delete File system call, or you can give it a new name with the Rename File system call.

Opening and Closing Files—Once a file has been created, there will be one or more directory entries on the disk for that file. In order to read or write any information, CP/M must know where the file resides on the disk (recall our example). It must, therefore, get that directory information from the disk into memory so that it can use the directory information. This is accomplished with the Open File system call. The Open File system call reads the information from the file's directory into the FCB contained in memory. *Prior* to issuing the Open File system call the FCB in memory for a file contains the file name and zeros in all other fields. *After* the Open File call is issued the remaining fields will be filed with data corresponding to the allocation map on the disk for our particular file. The allocation unit map has now been read from the disk directory entry and the FCB has been updated with this information.

CP/M will update the allocation unit map in *memory* in the FCB as it reads and writes new data to the file. Thus, when you are done updating the file, the new allocation unit map must be written back into the directory so that it will be permanently stored. This is accomplished with the Close File system call. While *reading* a file does not change the allocation unit map in any way (no records are being added or deleted if we are only reading), and therefore the allocation unit map in the directory will be the same as the one in memory, it is good programming practice to Close all files when you are done reading. If you write anything to a file you must always Close the file, or the new data may be lost.

Searching for a File—CP/M provides a method for determining if a file is on a disk. The Search File system call will return a zero (00H) value in the A register if the file named in the FCB is found on the disk. An FFH value is returned if the file is not present. In order to support ambiguous filenames, it is possible to place ASCII question marks ("?") in the filename in the FCB. If one or more question marks are encountered in the filename, then the Search File system call will return a 00H for the *first* filename that is a match. In order to find if there are other files that match, the Search Next File system call must be used. The Search Next File call will return a 00H for each file that matches the filename. When no more matches can be found, FFH is returned.

File Read and Write System Calls

Once a file has been properly opened, you may read and write data to the file. CP/M supports two basic kinds of read/write operations—*sequential* and *random access*. Sequential access is the simplest of the two, so we will examine it first.

Sequential Read/Write Operation—Sequential access allows your program to read or write successive records to a file. Once a file is opened, each successive read or write command will read or write the next record in the file. CP/M automatically updates the record number to be read or written every time a read or write system call is issued (byte 32 of FCB in Fig. A-1). Your program may set the initial extent and record to be read by setting bytes 12 and 32 in the FCB to the desired values. This way you can begin sequentially reading a file anywhere in that file without having to first read a lot of unwanted data. For example, if you had a file containing the monthly history of your balance sheet, and you wanted to start reading the July balances, you could position the extent and record count to the second half of the file so as to avoid reading the first six month's balances.

Despite sequential access's relative simplicity, it has some severe limitations which affect its use. In the above example, what would happen if we wanted to add a record (say a new account was added in August, and the balances had been left out of the history file) in the middle of the file. Every record after the one to be added would have to be read and rewritten, a very, very time consuming process in a large file. Because of this limitation (and other slightly less severe problems), the second method of access called random access is more commonly used.

Random Access—Random access allows you to read or write any record in a file without regard to what records, if any, come before or after it. CP/M 2.0 and later supports full random access records, whereas CP/M 1.4 and earlier support a kind of pseudorandom access. We will therefore consider the two separately.

CP/M 1.4 and earlier implement a kind of random access using the sequential access system call. As you may have noticed in the previous discussion, if we specify which extent and record we want read or written *every time* we issue a read or write system call, then we will have, in essence, random access capability. The restriction to this which keeps it from being true random access is the fact that under this scheme, if there are gaps in the records, the results can be unpredictable and troublesome. Consider, for example, what would happen under this method if we created a new file, opened it, wrote the 1st and 63rd records, closed it, reopened it, and attempted to read the 32nd record. Under CP/M 1.4 and earlier, the result that you would get back would be anything but the proper response, which would be that the desired record was not in the file. However, with this limitation (which is relatively easy to live with since very few applications would actually write the 1st and 63rd records with nothing in between) perfectly adequate random access reading and writing is possible.

CP/M 2.0 and later expanded on the random access capability of the earlier versions to where true random access is possible. Three new system calls, Read Random, Write Random, and Set Random Record were added. Random access using the sequential read/write commands, as was done under CP/M 1.4 and earlier, is still possible so that programs written under 1.4 and earlier can be run under version 2.0 and later.

However, the new Read Random and Write Random system calls have two enhancements which make true random access possible. The first is that records do not have to be contiguous, i.e., the example above with the 1st and 63rd record being written will be properly handled. The second enhancement, and by far the most useful, is CP/M's ability under 2.0 and later to convert record numbers from 1 to 65536 internally into the proper extent/record designations. This frees your program from having to convert say the 175th record in a file to 2nd extent, 47th record, as was required under earlier versions. In order to maintain compatibility with the earlier versions of CP/M, 2.0 and later place the random access record number in a three-byte field added to the tail end of the FCB (see the FCB layout in Fig. A-2).

The Set Random Record call facilitates the switching from sequential to random access in "midstream" so to speak, without losing your place. If, for example, your program had been merrily reading a file sequentially, and you suddenly decided to do some random access, this system call will set the random access record number (last three bytes in the 2.0 and later FCB) to the last record number read or written. (Remember, the read/write sequential calls will only update the extent and record bytes in the FCB, not the new random access record number bytes.)

Other Disk System Calls

Several other system calls are supported by CP/M which will greatly facilitate your use of the CP/M file structure in certain situations. They are used to initialize or interrogate certain disk functions.

The most commonly used of these is the Set DMA system call. This system call will set the disk i/o buffer to the 128 byte block of memory beginning with the address contained in the DE register pair. CP/M uses a default disk i/o buffer address of 0080H, but any 128-byte block of memory can be used. The Set DMA call is used whenever you would like to change the buffer.

The remaining system calls are used mainly by CP/M to implement the various disk related functions specified by the CP/M utilities.

Further Information

We have tried to present an overview here of some of the features of CP/M which are not readily apparent to the user, such as system calls. This has, however, been just an overview, and we strongly recommend that you read the CP/M manuals before you start doing any assembly language programming using system calls.

Appendix B

CP/M Compatible Software

This appendix presents an extensive, but still partial list of CP/M compatible programs and the companies that sell them. The list represents a condensed version of a survey put out by Small Systems Group (Box 5429, Santa Monica, CA, 90405). The complete survey can be purchased from Small Systems Group for $1.00 plus a stamped self-addressed envelope. The list here is divided into five program categories: accounting programs, general applications, industrial programs, utilities, and system programs. Within each of these five categories are further divisions to help keep the list clear. You can add to it as you desire. Under each heading is a name of the program product followed by the address of the program's vendor. Multiple addresses are included if one vendor has more than one product in the list to simplify your understanding of the companies and what they market. You can write to the company to gather information (specs, price, terms, etc.). A simple postcard will do. Note that you read about them in the CP/M Primer. A careful combing of the magazines: *Byte, Kilobaud, Creative Computing, On Computing,* and *Infoworld* will provide advertisements of the latest developments in CP/M software.

ACCOUNTING APPLICATIONS

Integrated Accounting

Program Name	*Vendor and Address*
Accounting Package	Aaron Associates Inc., Box 170A, Garden Grove, CA 92640
Complete Accounting	Micro Byte Computer Store, 2626 Union Avenue, San Jose, CA 95124
Moneybelt	Micro Source, 1425 W. 12th Place, Tempe, AZ 85281
Accounts Payable/Receivable	Osborne Associates, Inc., Box 2036, Berkeley, CA 94702
Integrated Business System	Serendipity Systems, 225 Elmira Rd., Ithaca, NY 14850
General Ledger	
General Ledger	Aaron Associates Inc., Box 170A, Garden Grove, CA 92640
General Ledger	BAS, 16755 Littlefield Lane, Los Gatos, CA 95030
General Ledger	California Microcomputer, Box 3199, Chico, CA 95927
Micro Ledger	CompuMax Associates, 505 Hamilton Avenue, Palo Alto, CA 94301
General Ledger	Data Train Inc., 840 N.W. 6th Street, Grants Pass, OR 97526
General Ledger	International Micro Systems, 3077 Merriman Lane, Kansas City, KS 66106
General Ledger	Micro Computer Consultants, Box 255625, Sacramento, CA 95825
Ledger Plus	Micro Source, 1425 W. 12th Place, Tempe, AZ 85281
General Ledger	Personal Software, 592 Weddell Drive, Sunnyvale, CA 94086
General Ledger	Serendipity Systems, 225 Elmira Rd., Ithaca, NY 14850
Payroll	
Payroll	Aaron Associates Inc., Box 170A, Garden Grove, CA 92640
Payroll	California Microcomputer, Box 3199, Chico, CA 95927

Program Name	*Vendor and Address*
Micro Pers	CompuMax Associates, 505 Hamilton Avenue, Palo Alto, CA 94301
Payroll	Graham Dorian Software Systems, 211 North Broadway, Wichita, KS 67202
Payroll	International Micro Systems, 3077 Merriam Lane, Kansas City, KS 66106
Payroll	Micro Data, 5622 Pacific Avenue, Olympia, WA 98503
Payroll	Personal Software, 592 Weddell Drive, Sunnyvale, CA 94086
Payroll (Personnel)	Serendipity Systems, 225 Elmira Rd., Ithaca, NY 14850
Accounts Payable	
Accounts Payable	BAS, 16755 Littlefield Lane, Los Gatos, CA 95030
Accounts Payable	Commercial Computer Inc., 9742 Humboldt Avenue, Minneapolis, MN 55431
Accounts Payable	Data Train Inc., 840 N.W. 6th Street, Grants Pass, OR 97526
Accounts Payable	Micro Byte Computer Store, 2626 Union Avenue, San Jose, CA 95124
Accounts Payable	Micro Data, 5622 Pacific Avenue, Olympia, WA 98503
Accounts Payable	Rothenberg Information Systems, 260 Sheridan Ave., Palo Alto, CA 94306
Accounts Payable	Serendipity Systems, 225 Elmira Rd., Ithaca, NY 14850
Accounts Receivable	
Accounts Receivable	Aaron Associates Inc., Box 170A, Garden Grove, CA 92640
Accounts Receivable	BAS, 16755 Littlefield Lane, Los Gatos, CA 95030
Balance Forward A/R	California Microcomputer, Box 3199, Chico, CA 95927
Microrec	CompuMax Associates, 505 Hamilton Avenue, Palo Alto, CA 94301
Accounts Receivable	H. H. Associates, Inc., Box 19504, Denver, CO 80219
Balance Forward A/R	International Micro Systems, 3077 Merriam Lane, Kansas City, KS 66106
Accounts Receivable	Micro Byte Computer Store, 2626 Union Avenue, San Jose, CA 95124
Accounts Receivable	Micro Data, 5622 Pacific Avenue, Olympia, WA 98503
Accounts Receivable	Personal Software, 592 Weddell Drive, Sunnyvale, CA 94086
Accounts Receivable	Structured Systems Group, 5208 Claremont Ave., Oakland, CA 94618
Billing	The Software Store, 706 Chippewa Square, Marquette, MI 49855
Accounts Receivable	Univair International, 10327 Lambert Intl. Airport, Saint Louis, MO 63145
Inventory	
Inventory	Aaron Associates Inc., Box 170A, Garden Grove, CA 92640
Microinv	CompuMax Associates, 505 Hamilton Avenue, Palo Alto, CA 94301
Inventory System	H. H. Associates, Inc., Box 19504, Denver, CO 80219
Inventory Control	International Micro Systems, 3077 Merriam Lane, Kansas City, KS 66106
Backorder Management	International Micro Systems, 3077 Merriam Lane, Kansas City, KS 66106
Mfr/Whlsale Inventory	Micro Computer Consultants, Box 255625, Sacramento, CA 95825
Inventory Management	Personal Software, 592 Weddell Drive, Sunnyvale, CA 94086
Retail Inventory	Serendipity Systems, 225 Elmira Rd., Ithaca, NY 14850
Order Entry	
Order Entry System	H. H. Associates, Inc., Box 19504, Denver, CO 80219

Program Name	*Vendor and Address*
Cash Disbursements	
Cash Disbursements	Aaron Associates Inc., Box 170A, Garden Grove, CA 92640
Cash Disbursements Posting	International Micro Systems, 3077 Merriam Lane, Kansas City, KS 66106
Cash Receipts	
Cash Register	Graham Dorian Software Systems, 211 North Broadway, Wichita, KS 67202
Job Costing	
Job Costing	Graham Dorian Software Systems, 211 North Broadway, Wichita, KS 67202
Fixed Assets Accounting	
Fixed Assets Accounting	Data Train Inc., 840 N.W. 6th Street, Grants Pass, OR 97526
	GENERAL APPLICATIONS
Data Base System	
Data Management System	Creative Computer Applications, 2218 Glenn Canyon Road, Altadena, CA 91001
Pearl	Computer Pathways Unlimited, 2151 Davcor Street, S.E., Salem, OR 97302
Global	Global Parameters, 1505 Ocean Avenue, Brooklyn, NY 11230
Categorical Information	H. H. Associates, Inc., Box 19504, Denver, CO 80219
Selector	Micro-Ap, 9807 Davona Drive, San Ramon, CA 94583
Midas	Rothenberg Information Systems, 260 Sheridan Ave., Palo Alto, CA 94306
Data Management	Univair International, 10327 Lambert Intl. Airport, Saint Louis, MO 63145
Text Editor	
Zedit	Computer Design Labs, 342 Columbus Avenue, Trenton, NJ 08629
Weed	Digital Marketing, 2670 Cherry Lane, Walnut Creek, CA 94596
Wordmaster	MicroPro International, 5810 Commerce Blvd., Rohnert Park, CA 94928
Text Editor	Software Ingenuity, Box 1964, Eugene, OR 97401
Text Editing System	Technical Systems Consultants, Box 2574, West Lafayette, IN 47906
Text Output Formatter	
Top	Computer Design Labs, 342 Columbus Avenue, Trenton, NJ 08629
Script 80 Professional	J. Vilkaitis, Box 26, High Street Extension, Thomaston, CT 06787
Textwriter	Organic Software, 1492 Windsor Way, Livermore, CA 94550
Text Processing System	Technical Systems Consultants, Box 2574, West Lafayette, IN 47906
Word Processor	
Idsword	CW Applications, 1776 E. Jefferson Street, Rockville, MD 20852
Pro-Type	Interactive Microwave Inc., Box 771, State College, PA 16801
Word Star	MicroPro International Corp., 1299 4th Street, San Rafael, CA 94901
WpDaisy	InfoSoft Systems Inc., 25 Sylvan Road South, Westport, CT 06880
Electric Pencil	Michael Shrayer Software, 1253 Viste Superba Dr., Glendale, CA 91205
Power Text	Personal Software, 592 Weddell Drive, Sunnyvale, CA 94086
The Magic Wand	Small Business Applications, 3220 Louisiana St., Houston, TX 77006

Program Name	Vendor and Address
Letteright	Structured Systems Group, 5208 Claremont Ave., Oakland, CA 94618
MWP/SEL	The Software Store, 706 Chippewa Square, Marquette, MI 49855
Mailing List System	
Mail List	Aaron Associates Inc., Box 170A, Garden Grove, CA 92640
Mail Listing	Commercial Computer Inc., 9742 Humboldt Avenue, Minneapolis, MN 55431
Mailing List Management	International Micro Systems, 3077 Merriam Lane, Kansas City, KS 66106
Mail Merge	InfoSoft Systems Inc., 25 Sylvan Road South, Westport, CT 06880
Postmaster	Lifeboat Associates, 1651 3rd Ave., New York, NY 10028
NAD	Structured Systems Group, 5208 Claremont Ave., Oakland, CA 94618
INDUSTRY APPLICATIONS	
Medical	
Automated Patient History	Cybernetics Inc., 8041 Newman Avenue, Huntington Beach, CA 92647
Medical Office Building	H. H. Associates, Inc., Box 19504, Denver, CO 80219
Medical Management	Univair International, 10327 Lambert Intl. Airport, Saint Louis, MO 63145
Legal	
Law Office Billing	H. H. Associates, Inc., Box 19504, Denver, CO 80219
Dental	
Dental Receivables	MBA Inc., Box 2528, Pasco, WA 99302
Construction	
House Cost Estimation Package	Business Information Systems, 7905 L Street, Omaha, NE 68129
Contractor Payroll	Micro Data, 5622 Pacific Avenue, Olympia, WA 98503
Property Management	
Property Management	A-T Enterprises, 221 North Lois, La Habra, CA 90631
Apartment Management	H. H. Associates, Inc., Box 19504, Denver, CO 80219
Cash Flow	Realty Software Inc., 2126 Lombard Street, San Francisco, CA 94123
Membership Billing	
Country Club Receivables	MBA Inc., Box 2528, Pasco, WA 99302
Utility Billing	
Utility Billing	Micro Data, 5622 Pacific Avenue, Olympia, WA 98503
Golf Club	
Golf Handicap	Micro Data, 5622 Pacific Avenue, Olympia, WA 98503
Insurance Agent	
Insurance Agent	Micro Data, 5622 Pacific Avenue, Olympia, WA 98503
Lumber Company	
Log/Lumber Inventory	Micro Data, 5622 Pacific Avenue, Olympia, WA 98503
Accounting	
Master Tax	CPAids, 1640 Franklin Avenue, Kent, OH 44240
CPA G/L and Client Statement	MBA Inc., Box 2528, Pasco, WA 99302
Professional	
Integrated Professional Office	Serendipity Systems, 225 Elmira Rd., Ithaca, NY 14850
Professional Client Billing	Serendipity Systems, 225 Elmira Rd., Ithaca, NY 14850

Program Name	Vendor and Address
Medical or Dental	
Integrated Med/Dental Office	Serendipity Systems, 225 Elmira Rd., Ithaca, NY 14850
Medical/Dental Patient Billing	Serendipity Systems, 225 Elmira Rd., Ithaca, NY 14850
School Administration	
Student Records and Scheduling	International Micro Systems, 3077 Merriam Lane, Kansas City, KS 66106
Engineering	
Control Systems Analysis	Compco, 8705 North Port Washington Rd., Milwaukee, WI 53217
Bowling Alley	
Bowling Bookeeper	Compco, 8705 North Port Washington Rd., Milwaukee, WI 53217
	UTILITY APPLICATIONS
Mathematical Routine	
Development Utilities	Allen Ashley, 395 Sierra Madre Villa, Pasadena, CA 91107
Floating Point Package	Southern Systems of Birmingham, Box 3373-A, Birmingham, AL 35205
Statistical Package	
Statistics	Basic Business Software, Box 2032, Salt Lake City, UT 84110
Statpak	Northwest Analytical, Box 14430, Portland, OR 97214
ISAM Package	
Kiss	EIDOS Systems Corp., 315 Wilhagan Rd., Nashville, TN 37217
Graphics	
Graphic Subroutine Package	Compco, 8705 North Port Washington Rd., Milwaukee, WI 53217
Plotting	
Plotting	Basic Business Software, Box 2032, Salt Lake City, UT 84110
Finance	
Finance Calculator	Basic Business Software, Box 2032, Salt Lake City, UT 84110
Communication	
Download	Cybernetics Inc., 8041 Newman Avenue, Huntington Beach, CA 92647
Mcall	Micro Call Services, 9655-M Homestead Court, Laurel, MD 20810
Intelligent Terminal	InfoSoft Systems Inc., 25 Sylvan Road South, Westport, CT 06880
Screen Editor	
Daisy	InfoSoft Systems Inc., 25 Sylvan Road South, Westport, CT 06880
Forms-2	Micro Focus Ltd., 1601 Civic Center Drive, Santa Clara, CA 95050
Form Production	
Automated Forms Control	H. H. Associates, Inc., Box 19504, Denver, CO 80219
Print Spooler	
Despool	Digital Research, Box 579, Pacific Grove, CA 93950
Spool	InfoSoft Systems Inc., 25 Sylvan Road South, Westport, CT 06880
Sort	
Super Sort	MicroPro International, 5810 Commerce Blvd., Rohnert Park, CA 94928
Multi Key Sort	Rothenberg Information Systems, 260 Sheridan Ave., Palo Alto, CA 94306

Program Name	Vendor and Address
Sort	The Software Store, 706 Chippewa Square, Marquette, MI 49855
SYSTEMS PROGRAMS	
Development Systems	
PDS-Program Development System	Allen Ashley, 395 Sierra Madre Villa, Pasadena, CA 91107
I/SAL	InfoSoft Systems Inc., 25 Sylvan Road South, Westport, CT 06880
Z-80 Development Package	Lifeboat Associates, 1651 3rd Ave., New York, NY 10028
Low Precision Basic	Computer Design Labs., 342 Columbus Avenue, Trenton, NJ 08629
Business Basic	Computer Design Labs, 342 Columbus Avenue, Trenton, NJ 08629
UCSD Pascal	Digimedics, 501 Cedar Street, Santa Cruz, CA 95060
Basic Compiler	Interactive Microwave Inc., Box 771, State College. PA 16801
ALGOL 60 Compiler (Z-80)	Lifeboat Associates, 1651 3rd Ave., New York, NY 10028
CIS COBOL Compact	Micro Focus Ltd., 1601 Civic Center Drive, Santa Clara, CA 95050
Basic Compiler	Microsoft, 10800 NE Eighth, Bellevue, WA 98004
COBOL-80	Microsoft, 10800 NE Eighth, Bellevue, WA 98004
CBASIC	Software Systems, Box 145, Sierra Madre, CA 91024
Tarbell Basic	Tarbell Electronics, 950 Dovlen Place, Carson, CA 90746
APL Interpreter	Vanguard Systems Corp., 6712 San Pedro Avenue, San Antonio, TX 78216
Assembler	
XMAC 6800	Allen Ashley, 395 Sierra Madre Villa, Pasadena, CA 91107
MAC	Digital Research, Box 579, Pacific Grove, CA 93950
8048 Cross Assembler	Software Ingenuity, Box 1964, Eugene, OR 97401
RLSAM	InfoSoft Systems Inc., 25 Sylvan Road South, Westport, CT 06880
A-Natural Assembler	Whitesmiths Ltd., 127 E. 59th Street, New York, NY 10022
Debugging Monitor	
DEBUG	Computer Design Labs, 342 Columbus Avenue, Trenton, NJ 08629
DEB	InfoSoft Systems Inc., 25 Sylvan Road South, Westport, CT 06880
SID	Digital Research, Box 579, Pacific Grove, CA 93950
Utility Program	
Z80/8080 Disassembler	Affordable Computers, 16508 Hawthorne Blvd., Lawndale, CA 90260
Transfer	Computer Services, 30 Hwy., 321, NW, Hickory, NC 28601
DISLOG	Lifeboat Associates, 1651 3rd Ave., New York, NY 10028
Expander	MICAH, P.O. Box 22212, San Francisco, CA 94122
IBM-CP/M File Conversion	Smith Computer Systems, 530 Pierce Avenue, Dyer, IN 46311
TTY Model 40 Printer Interface	Smith Computer Systems, 530 Pierce Avenue, Dyer, IN 46311
DISK Utility	The Software Store, 706 Chippewa Square, Marquette, MI 49855
PRGM/MAP	The Software Store, 706 Chippewa Square, Marquette, MI 49855
Librarian	Whitesmiths Ltd., 127 E. 59th Street, New York, NY 10022
REL	Whitesmiths Ltd., 127 E. 59th Street, New York, NY 10022
Loader	
Linker	Computer Design Labs, 342 Columbus Avenue, Trenton. NJ 08629
LINKA	InfoSoft Systems Inc., 25 Sylvan Road South, Westport, CT 06880

Courtesy Small Systems Group

Appendix **C**

CP/M Reference

RESIDENT COMMANDS

Command	Description
DIR	Type a directory of the current disk.
DIR ufn	Check for a file on the current disk.
DIR afn	Check for one or more files on the current disk.
ERA ufn	Erase a file from the current disk.
ERA afn	Erase one or more files from the current disk.
REN ufn=ufn,..,ufn=ufn	Rename one or more files. New filename is left of equal sign and old filename is to the right.
SAVE n ufn	Save n 256 byte blocks of memory in a file on the current disk.
TYPE ufn,ufn,..,ufn	Type one or more files to the console.

Note: An optional disk drive reference can be inserted before any ufn (d:ufn) or afn (d:afn) if the file or files desired are not on the current disk. In the above examples, ufn means unambiguous filename and afn means ambiguous filename. The "?" is the single character wildcard, and "*" is the "fill right with "?'s" wildcard. Filenames may have up to eight characters in them, and file types may have up to three.

UTILITIES

STAT Check Status

Command	Description
STAT	Returns the amount of unused space on the currently logged disk.
STAT x:	Returns the amount of unused space on drive x:.
STAT ufn	Returns the size in bytes, records, and extents of file ufn.
STAT afn	Returns the size in bytes, records, and extents of the files that match afn.
STAT x:=R/O	Sets drive x: as read only.
STAT val:	Returns the possible logical-physical assignments for the four i/o devices.
STAT dev:	Returns the current logical-physical assignments for the four i/o devices.
STAT ld:=pd:	Assigns logical device ld: as physical device pd:.
STAT dsk:	Returns the current disks logged on to the system.

PIP Transfer Files

Command	Description
PIP y:=x:ufn	Transfer a file, ufn from one drive x: to another drive y:.
PIP y:=x:afn	Transfer one or more files that match the afn from drive x: to drive y:.
PIP y:ufn1=x:ufn2	Transfer a file, ufn2 from drive x: to drive y: and rename it ufn1.

MOVCPM Relocate System Image

Command	Description
MOVCPM*	Relocates the system image size to utilize all available memory.
MOVCPMn*	Relocates the system image to utilize nK bytes of memory.

Note: The "*" instructs MOVCPM to leave the new system image in memory (for subsequent use by SYSMOV). If the "*" is left out, the system image is moved to the disk that was last booted off of.

SYSGEN Generate a CP/M System

SYSGEN Initiates the SYSGEN dialog.

ED Edit a File

ED ufn Load ED into memory and open the file specified by the ufn.

Commands:

Command	Description
nA	Append n lines of text.
E	End edit.
nF<Text>	Find <Text> n times.
H	Save and reedit file.
I	Insert text.
nM<Comd Str>	Repeat the command string n times.
nN<Text>	Search for the nth occurrence of <Text> with Appends and Writes where necessary.
Q	Abandon edited text and restart editing session.
O	Abandon edited text and restore original source file then exit edit.
Rufn	Insert file ufn from library.
nS<OT> Z<NT>	Search for old text <OT> and replace with new text <NT> n times.*
U	Convert all input from lower case to upper case.
nW	Write n lines of text.

+/−B	Move CP to beginning or end of buffer.
+/−nC	Move CP +/− n characters.
+/−nD	Delete n characters ahead of or behind CP.
+/−nK	Kill n lines ahead of or behind CP.
+/−nL	Move CP +/−n lines in the buffer.
+/−nT	Type the previous or next n lines in the buffer.
+/−n	Move forward or backward n lines in the buffer and then type that line.

*Note: Z = Control Z.

ASM Assemble a File

ASM filename.abc — Assemble FILENAME.ASN with xyz as optional parameters as follows:
a: disk drive of source file.
b: disk drive of .HEX file or Z if .HEX file to be suppressed.
c: disk drive of .PRN file or X if listing to be sent to console or Z if .PRN file to be suppressed.

Constants:

B = binary	D = decimal
O or Q = octal	H = hexadecimal

Operators:

x + y	Unsigned arithmetic sum of x and y.
x − y	Unsigned arithmetic difference of x and y.
+ y	Unary plus.
− y	Unary minus.
x * y	Unsigned multiplication of x and y.
x / y	Unsigned division of x by y.
x MOD y	Remainder after x / y.
NOT y	Logical inverse of y.
x AND y	Bit-by-bit logical AND of x and y.
x OR y	Bit-by-bit logical OR of x and y.
x XOR y	Bit-by-bit logical EXCLUSIVE OR of x and y.
x SHL y	Shift x left y bits with zero fill.
x SHR y	Shift x right y bits with zero fill.

Assembler Directives:

ORG	Define starting address of the program or data section.
END	End program assembly.
EQU	Define a numeric constant.
SET	Set a numeric value.
IF	Begin conditional assembly.
ENDIF	End conditional assembly.
DB	Define data byte.
DW	Define data word.
DS	Define data storage area.

DDT Debug a File

DDT ufn — Load DDT into memory. Optional filename is loaded into the default FCB (File Control Block) for future —R (Read) commands.

Commands:

Aa	Assemble code starting at address a.
Ds,f	Display memory from optional starting address s to optional ending address f.
Fs,f,d	Fill memory from starting address s through ending address f with hexadecimal value d.
G,a	Begin program execution, independent of DDT, with optional breakpoint at address a.
Iafn	Insert filename into the default FCB for future —R commands.
Ls,f	List a program from optional starting address s to optional ending address f.
Ms,f,d	Move a block of data starting with address s and ending with address f to a new memory block beginning with address d.
R	Read the file whose filename is in the default FCB into memory.
Sa	Set the byte contained in memory location a to a new value.
Tn	Trace n program steps.
Un	Untrace n program steps.
Xr	Examine and modify CPU register r.

LOAD Convert Hex to Com File

LOAD ufn — Load reads a .HEX file created with ASM and creates a .COM file.

Index

T

U

V

W

X

TO THE READER

Sams Computer books cover Fundamentals — Programming — Interfacing — Technology written to meet the needs of computer engineers, professionals, scientists, technicians, students, educators, business owners, personal computerists and home hobbyists.

Our Tradition is to meet your needs and in so doing we invite you to tell us what your needs and interests are by completing the following:

1. I need books on the following topics:

____

____

____

____

____

____

____

____

2. I have the following Sams titles:

____

____

____

____

____

____

____

____

3. My occupation is:

_____ Scientist, Engineer	_____ D P Professional
_____ Personal computerist	_____ Business owner
_____ Technician, Serviceman	_____ Computer store owner
_____ Educator	_____ Home hobbyist
_____ Student	Other ______________________

Name (print)______________________________

Address______________________________

City ______________________ State ____________ Zip ____________

Mail to: **Howard W. Sams & Co., Inc.**
Marketing Dept. #CBS1/80
4300 W. 62nd St., P.O. Box 7092
Indianapolis, Indiana 46206

—CUT HERE — FOLD HERE —

CP/M Reference Card

by

Stephen M. Murtha and Mitchell Waite

RESIDENT COMMANDS

Command	Description
DIR	Type a directory of the current disk.
DIR ufn	Check for a file on the current disk.
DIR afn	Check for one or more files on the current disk.
ERA ufn	Erase a file from the current disk.
ERA afn	Erase one or more files from the current disk.
REN ufn=ufn,..,ufn=ufn	Rename one or more files. New filename is left of equal sign and old filename is to the right.
SAVE n ufn	Save n 256 byte blocks of memory in a file on the current disk.
TYPE ufn,ufn,..,ufn	Type one or more files to the console.

Note: An optional disk drive reference can be inserted before any ufn (d:ufn) or afn (d:afn) if the file or files desired are not on the current disk. In the above examples, ufn means unambiguous filename and afn means ambiguous filename. The "?" is the single character wildcard, and "*" is the "fill right with "?'s" wildcard. Filenames may have up to eight characters in them, and file types may have up to three.

UTILITIES

STAT Check Status

Command	Description
STAT	Returns the amount of unused space on the currently logged disk.
STAT x:	Returns the amount of unused space on drive x:.
STAT ufn	Returns the size in bytes, records, and extents of file ufn.
STAT afn	Returns the size in bytes, records, and extents of the files that match afn.
STAT x:=R/O	Sets drive x: as read only.
STAT val:	Returns the possible logical-physical assignments for the four i/o devices.
STAT dev:	Returns the current logical-physical assignments for the four i/o devices.
STAT ld:=pd:	Assigns logical device ld: as physical device pd:.
STAT dsk:	Returns the current disks logged on to the system.

PIP Transfer Files

Command	Description
PIP y:=x:ufn	Transfer a file, ufn from one drive x: to another drive y:.
PIP y:=x:afn	Transfer one or more files that match the afn from drive x: to drive y:.
PIP y:ufn1=x:ufn2	Transfer a file, ufn2 from drive x: to drive y: and rename it ufn1.

MOVCPM Relocate System Image

Command	Description
MOVCPM*	Relocates the system image size to utilize all available memory.
MOVCPMn*	Relocates the system image to utilize nK bytes of memory.

Note: The "*" instructs MOVCPM to leave the new system image in memory (for subsequent use by SYSMOV). If the "*" is left out, the system image is moved to the disk that was last booted off of.

SYSGEN Generate a CP/M System

SYSGEN Initiates the SYSGEN dialog.

ED Edit a File

ED ufn Load ED into memory and open the file specified by the ufn.

Commands:

Command	Description
nA	Append n lines of text.
E	End edit.
nF<Text>	Find <Text> n times.
H	Save and reedit file.
I	Insert text.
nM<Comd Str>	Repeat the command string n times.
nN<Text>	Search for the nth occurrence of <Text> with Appends and Writes where necessary.
Q	Abandon edited text and restart editing session.
O	Abandon edited text and restore original source file then exit edit.
Rufn	Insert file ufn from library.
nS<OT> Z<NT>	Search for old text <OT> and replace with new text <NT> n times.*
U	Convert all input from lower case to upper case.
nW	Write n lines of text.
+/−B	Move CP to beginning or end of buffer.
+/−nC	Move CP +/− n characters.
+/−nD	Delete n characters ahead of or behind CP.
+/−nK	Kill n lines ahead of or behind CP.
+/−nL	Move CP +/−n lines in the buffer.
+/−nT	Type the previous or next n lines in the buffer.
+/−n	Move forward or backward n lines in the buffer and then type that line.

*Note: Z = Control Z.

ASM Assemble a File

ASM filename.abc Assemble FILENAME.ASN with xyz as optional parameters as follows:
a: disk drive of source file.
b: disk drive of .HEX file or Z if .HEX file to be suppressed.
c: disk drive of .PRN file or X if listing to be sent to console or Z if .PRN file to be suppressed.

Constants:

B = binary	D = decimal
O or Q = octal	H = hexadecimal

Operators:

x + y	Unsigned arithmetic sum of x and y.
x − y	Unsigned arithmetic difference of x and y.
+ y	Unary plus.
− y	Unary minus.
x * y	Unsigned multiplication of x and y.
x / y	Unsigned division of x by y.
x MOD y	Remainder after x / y.
NOT y	Logical inverse of y.
x AND y	Bit-by-bit logical AND of x and y.
x OR y	Bit-by-bit logical OR of x and y.
x XOR y	Bit-by-bit logical EXCLUSIVE OR of x and y.
x SHL y	Shift x left y bits with zero fill.
x SHR y	Shift x right y bits with zero fill.

Assembler Directives:

ORG	Define starting address of the program or data section.
END	End program assembly.
EQU	Define a numeric constant.
SET	Set a numeric value.
IF	Begin conditional assembly.
ENDIF	End conditional assembly.
DB	Define data byte.
DW	Define data word.
DS	Define data storage area.

DDT Debug a File

DDT ufn Load DDT into memory. Optional filename is loaded into the default FCB (File Control Block) for future −R (Read) commands.

Commands:

Aa	Assemble code starting at address a.
Ds,f	Display memory from optional starting address s to optional ending address f.
Fs,f,d	Fill memory from starting address s through ending address f with hexadecimal value d.
G,a	Begin program execution, independent of DDT, with optional breakpoint at address a.
Iafn	Insert filename into the default FCB for future −R commands.
Ls,f	List a program from optional starting address s to optional ending address f.
Ms,f,d	Move a block of data starting with address s and ending with address f to a new memory block beginning with address d.
R	Read the file whose filename is in the default FCB into memory.
Sa	Set the byte contained in memory location a to a new value.
Tn	Trace n program steps.
Un	Untrace n program steps.
Xr	Examine and modify CPU register r.

LOAD Convert Hex to Com File

LOAD ufn Load reads a .HEX file created with ASM and creates a .COM file.

Notes

Notes